# Open Systems
# For Europe

## UNICOM Applied Information Technology Reports

UNICOM Applied Information Technology Reports form a series of books, each of which is based upon papers given at a seminar organized by UNICOM Seminars Ltd. The reports cover subjects at the forefront of information technology, and the contributors are all authorities in the subject on which they are invited to write, either as researchers or as practitioners.

1    **Fourth-Generation Systems**
     **Their scope, application and methods of evaluation**
     Edited by Simon Holloway

2    **Evaluating Supercomputers**
     **Strategies for exploiting, evaluating and benchmarking**
     Edited by A. van der Steen

3    **Failsafe Control Systems**
     **Applications and emergency management**
     Edited by Kevin Warwick and Ming T. Tham

4    **Computer Vision and Image Processing**
     Edited by Anthony Barrett

5    **The Distributed Development Environment**
     **The art of using CASE**
     Edited by Simon Holloway

6    **Software Quality and Reliability**
     **Tools and methods**
     Edited by Darrel Ince

7    **Open Systems for Europe**
     Edited by Tony Elliman and Colston Sanger

8    **Hypermedia/Hypertext**
     **And Object-oriented Databases**
     Edited by Heather Brown

# Open Systems For Europe

UNICOM

APPLIED INFORMATION TECHNOLOGY REPORTS 7

Edited by **Tony Elliman**

*Senior Lecturer in Computer Science, Brunel University*

and

**Colston Sanger**

*Senior Consultant, Gid Ltd*

*Springer-Science+Business Media, B.V.*

First edition 1991

© 1991 Springer Science+Business Media Dordrecht
Originally published by Chapman & Hall in 1991
Softcover reprint of the hardcover 1st edition 1991

**British Library Cataloguing in Publication Data**
Open systems for Europe. – (Unicom applied information technology
   reports).
  1. Open computer systems
  I. Elliman, T.   II. Sanger, C.   III. Series
  004.62

  ISBN 978-0-412-37850-8          ISBN 978-1-4899-3073-6 (eBook)
  DOI 10.1007/978-1-4899-3073-6


**Library of Congress Cataloging-in-Publication Data**
Open systems for Europe / edited by T. Elliman and C. Sanger. — 1st
   ed.
       p.     cm. — (Unicom applied information technology reports)
   Includes bibliographical references.
   ISBN 978-0-412-37850-8
   1. Information technology—Standards—European Economic Community
countries.   2. Europe 1992.   I. Elliman, T. (Tony), 1947–
II. Sanger, C. (Colston), 1950–        III. Series.
HC240.9.I55064   1991
338.4'7004'094—dc20                                          90-20978
                                                                 CIP

# CONTENTS

# CONTRIBUTORS

**M. Anstee**
System Director
LIBC

**W. de Backer**
Director of Informatics
Commission of the European
Communities

**W.L. Bedford**
Purchasing Suppliers System
British Coal

**P.J. Bishop**
National Health Service Centre for
Information Technology

**N. Bush**
Senior Consultant
SEMA Group PLC

**L. Caffrey**
CCTA

**C.V. Calder**
AA Computing and Communications

**M. Eaton**
Finance, Product and Marketing
Manager
Relational Technology Ltd

**A.D. Elliman**
Dept of Computer Science
Brunel University

**W. Greaves**
IT Standards Unit
DTI

**S. Hammarling**
The Numerical Algorithms Group Ltd

**C. Lazou**
University of London
Computing Centre

**R.A. Matthews**
Director Network Systems
ICL

**P.W.L. Morgan**
Director Corporate Services
IBM UK Ltd

**A. Twigger**
Director of Consultancy
Unisoft Ltd

**C. Sanger**
Senior Consultant
Gid Ltd

**B. Wood**
SEMA Group PLC

# ACKNOWLEDGEMENTS

This book grew out of a conference, *Open Systems for Europe: towards 1992* organised by Unicom Seminars Ltd in collaboration with Unigram in December 1988. Because of limitations of space it has not been possible to reproduce all the contributions to that conference here, but we hope we have represented the substance of the debate. Thanks are due to all the speakers and contributors to this volume, and also to: Roy Barnes of LAMSAC; Marco d'Angelantonio and Lance English, then of Olivetti Systems & Networks UK; Pamela Gray, then of Sphinx; Peter Griffiths of The Instruction Set; Claude Hamon of Groupe Bull; Henning Oldenburg, then of the Open Software Foundation; and Dr Ing. Alessandro Osnaghi of the Direzione Formazione Olivetti Systems & Networks.

Our especial thanks go to Basil Cousins of Olivetti Systems & Networks UK, the conference chairman, who also arranged the live demonstration of Open Systems networking that was a feature of the conference.

# INTRODUCTION

# Open Systems for Europe

*A.D. Elliman, C. Sanger*

Open Systems for Europe combines two important and topical themes. First, Open Systems – the development of vendor-independent means to link and interwork with applications across a range of different systems. Secondly, the formation of a single European market after 1992 with its attendant opening up of public purchasing and the removal of the remaining obstacles to the free movement of products, people and services between the member states of the European Community.

What unites these two themes is the issue of standards. As Walter de Backer, Director of Informatics of the Commission of the European Communities (CEC) says in his keynote paper [Ch.1], more and more organisations are beginning to realise that an IT strategy based on standards is feasible, economic and necessary. It is feasible, if not immediately, then certainly through an evolutionary path phased over a number of years; it is economic because the costs associated with interface changes and conversions can be avoided, if not eliminated totally; and it is necessary if organisations are to communicate and interwork effectively. Moreover, the restructuring of Europe into a single market has already prompted a realignment of corporate interests – existing groups are breaking up and forming new, pan-European conglomerates. The successful organisations, those that continue to prosper and grow in the open Europe beyond 1992, will without doubt require standards if effective interworking between their new partners and across national boundaries is to be achieved. Turning to the supplier's view, it is evident that standardisation has a multiplier effect. As more people communicate with each other and more services are able to interwork, so the volume of information that is exchanged increases – and thus the larger the IT market becomes.

The natural audience for this book, therefore, includes IT managers, purchasing or procurement officers and all those within user organisations who seek to justify the business case for an Open Systems IT strategy. In addition, at the technical level, system designers and implementation managers will find much of interest by way of discussion of functional standardisation and guidelines and checklists for the successful completion of Open Systems projects. This book also provides an important resource for students of information systems development and computer science who need to gain an insight into the effect of market forces and the role of standards in system procurement. Finally, suppliers' representatives will undoubtedly search these pages for marketing opportunities and fresh ways of presenting their sales arguments.

## The structure of this book

The book is divided into four parts. Part One consists of the keynote papers from government agencies. These are presented by representatives of the CEC and the UK Department of Trade and Industry (DTI) and Central Computer and Telecommunications Agency (CCTA). In Part Two the suppliers present their views of the developing market and the role of standards, extrapolating and extending the already established themes. Part Three consists of user case studies. Here you will find the crux of the business argument for Open Systems, together with lessons learnt and benefits realised. Part Four is mainly concerned with software issues and ends with a valuable discussion of conformance testing and software verification. Each part comments on and develops ideas from the others. This structure is pragmatic rather than strictly logical and it makes sense, therefore, to discuss the individual contributions in terms of several overarching themes.

## OSI standards are not enough

The first theme is that standards for Open Systems Interconnection (OSI) are not enough. Certainly, OSI is the backbone of the Open Systems concept and, as Bush and Wood make clear [Ch.5], it is now a maturing activity, both in terms of the development of the standards themselves and their use in IT systems and related equipment. Of the initial set required by the International Standards Organisation (ISO) in its famous – perhaps one should say infamous – seven-layer reference model, standards corresponding to layers 1–4 are now agreed. These cover access to sub-networks (i.e. LAN's and X.25-based WANs) and the Network and Transport services. Standards for layers 5 and 6, the Session and Presentation layers, have also been published by ISO. Finally, standards for layer 7, the Application layer, have been agreed in four areas: for File Transfer, Access and Management (FTAM), for X.400 messaging, for remote terminal access (the Virtual Terminal Standards) and for Job Transfer and Manipulation (the JTM standards). Supplementing these is the multi-part Office Document Architecture (ODA) standard.

What is increasingly evident, however, is that work is required to flesh out and consolidate this initial set of standards. On the one hand, they require extensions either as in the case of layers 1–4, for example, to address new LAN technologies such as Fibre Distributed Data Interface (FDDI) or, as in the case of FTAM, to provide more sophisticated facilities in response to the needs of distributed office applications. On the other hand, there are related aspects such as network configuration and management, security and directory services that also need to be adressed. All of this is quite apart from the need to extend the standards-making agenda to include yet other urgent topics such as the harmonisation of the X/OPEN Common Application Environment (CAE) and the POSIX standards, and the definition of standards for transaction processing, for interactive access to remote or distributed databases, for graphics and for the human-computer interface. All of these – as is pointed out by de Backer (Ch.1], Bush and Wood [Ch.5], and Eaton [Ch.6] – involve much wider issues than those addressed by the present set of OSI standards.

International standards, by nature, attempt to be all things to all people. Given the number of countries, pressure groups and vested interests involved in the creation of an international standard, it is no wonder that they are essentially a compromise covering a wide range of technologies and possible applications. They include optional features and various choices of parameters. This complexity introduces the risk not only of differing interpretations, but also substantially different and incompatible implementations by the suppliers. In the mid-1980s, therefore, so-called **functional standards** (sometimes known as profiles) began to appear as the counterpart of the **base standards** referred to above.

Developed originally by suppliers' groups such as the Standards Promotion and Application Group (SPAG) in Europe, but later taken up by CEN/CENELEC (Committee for European Normalisation/Electro-Technical Division), functional standards are not new base standards: rather they are a tool for the practical implementation of OSI-based products. They are not completely option-free, but care is taken to include only those options that can be freely chosen, without disturbing the basic interworking between different suppliers' implementations. The most well-known are probably MAP (Manufacturing Automation Protocol) and TOP (Technical Office Protocol) pioneered by General Motors and Boeing in the early 1980s. Another is GOSIP (Government OSI Profile) discussed here by Caffrey [Ch.3] – although GOSIP is sometimes seen as a procurement rather than a functional standard, which seeks to define a minimum requirement that suppliers should meet as a prerequisite for selling to government organisations. Over the next few years, other functional standards will undoubtedly emerge to meet particular industrial and commercial requirements.

## An architecture is more than standards

The second theme, again introduced by de Backer [Ch.1], is that an architecture is more than standards. An organisation's IT architecture is, necessarily, based on more than simply technical standards. It is developed from the organisation's business strategy; and the decisions in which it is grounded are economic, functional and technical – not least because in its implementation, organisations must use commercially-available products and must therefore make informed guesses on when such products will become available.

An interesting and relevant point here, raised by both Calder [Ch.8] and Bishop [Ch.9], is the management of non-conformance. An Open Systems IT strategy is not a panacea – in any organisation there will be occasions when a pragmatic, non-OSI standard, non-strategic solution is the only answer. In this connection, Morgan [Ch.7] gives a cogent argument for the use of proprietary systems where advanced functionality and performance are important. Organisational growth by acquisition poses similar problems of non-conformance: how can acquired systems, that have not followed an Open Systems strategy, be integrated into the overall IT architecture?

## The business case for Open Systems

The third theme of this book is arguably the most crucial: the business case for Open Systems.

No-one should underestimate the amount of effort involved or the challenge to organisational inertia posed by adopting an Open Systems IT strategy. It is not a trival task. It cannot be achieved overnight or by mandate. As Calder, Bishop, Anstee and Bedford all make abundantly clear in Part Three, there will be change, risk and uncertainty. At the technical level, it is likely that an organisation will have to change the way in which it recruits, trains and manages its IT staff. At the broader, organisational level, as the riches of the organisation's information base become readily available on every desktop, and as electronic messaging frees up the lines of communication, it will change working practices. Indeed, it will change the way the organisation itself does business. Not everyone will welcome these changes.

To be sure, top management commitment is vital, but since the changes will affect everybody, everybody must both know about and be behind the strategy. Far from being just another piece of paper or report to be skimmed and then filed, an organisation's Open Systems IT strategy represents a consensus of agreement to a set of goals and the means of achieving them. It is, moreover, a living thing: a continuously evolving process of refinement and reassessment.

Equally, however, the benefits of Open Systems are plain for all to see. IT is increasingly the life-blood of all organisations. Flexibility and responsiveness to changing market conditions are the key issues. Growing IT budgets mean that financial control and return on investment is essential. Apart from long-term cost savings, Open Systems standards mean the end of dependence on a single supplier, to be replaced by competitive tendering and the purchase of what are increasingly becoming commodity products is an open market-place. They mean the protection of IT investment and reduced risk of obsolescence, together with the ability to expand in directions not originally envisaged. Most of all, by facilitating the multiple use of its workstations and of its data communications network, Open Systems products enable an organisation to introduce new systems and services at marginal incremental cost, but with maximum added value. Open Systems are therefore not just desirable, they are directly relevant today.

# ABSTRACTS

## 1  Guidelines for an informatics architecture

*W. de Backer, CEC*

As a user of Information Technology (IT) for its own administration the Commission of the European Communities (CEC) has been – as it has to be – a forerunner and an example in applying a procurement policy based on standards. The CEC adopted this policy in 1980.

In order to share its experience with other customers, the IT industry and the standard-making bodies, the CEC is publishing this third edition of its guidelines for the implementation of a vendor-independent architecture.

These guidelines will be revised regularly to respond to changes in the market place. Since the first edition in February 1985, there has been considerable progress in the area of standardisation and a significant shift among major customers towards adopting standardised products.

This edition incorporates further developments to the architecture with a particular emphasis on simplicity, economy, timing and end-user services. Options left open for the future in the last edition have now been settled: inter-institutional cooperation (INSIS and CADDIA), ISDN, LAN, cabling, addressing, security, interactive communication, file transfer, applications architecture. Parts of the previous edition have been rewritten, without however changing the substance.

The next edition of these guidelines will concentrate on applications architecture. The Commission of the European Communities would be grateful to receive information and suggestions.

## 2  UK Government programmes to encourage Open Systems

*W. Greaves, DTI*

This chapter is in three parts. The outline of UK Government programme presented by Warren Greaves is followed by a DTI status report on the OSI Opportunity Studies activity and a list of the participants as at the end of 1988.

## 3  Towards a European GOSIP

*L. Caffrey, CCTA*

This chapter provides a brief introduction to an evolving European OSI profile, currently known as EPHOS. A European Procurement Handbook for Open Systems will provide guidelines to public purchasers for OSI products in Europe. The work is being progressed by people from the United Kingdom,

French and German public administrations who believe that OSI profiles and standards do not on their own provide sufficient precision for public procurement purposes. EPHOS is therefore intended to provide to public sector purchasers information to assist them to buy Open IT Systems within the requirements of European Legislation.

This chapter sets out the role of CCTA and its involvement in OSI leading to the EPHOS development of the project; why the project is necessary, and what can be achieved through it.

## 4   Open Systems Interconnection: gaining a foothold in Europe through standards

*R.A. Matthews, ICL*

This chapter describes the initiatives which have driven the International Functional Standardisation activity and the ICL policy for their adoption and programmed use to provide practical migration paths from current proprietary interconnections to all OSI solutions.

The mood of users has switched from tired scepticism about OSI to the acceptance of its demonstrable success and a keen desire to develop their plans for Migration to OSI.

OSI solutions will dominate the European and global markets of the 1990s.

## 5   Standardisation for Open Systems Interconnection: recent developments and future directions

*N. Bush and B. Wood, SEMA*

This chapter provides an overview of the current state of work on standardisation for Open Systems Interconnection, covering work which is nearing completion, major areas of current development, and functional standardisation. It also looks at future directions for standardisation, such as work on open distributed processing (ODP).

## 6   Relational database opportunities within the single European market: commitment to standards and open systems

*M. Eaton, RTI – Ingres Ltd*

The creation of a single European market in 1992 will generate significant trading opportunities and challenges for UK companies. All businesses wanting to take full advantage of these opportunities cannot afford to ignore the market's technology requirements and if they have not already done so, must start to address these requirements in the light of their own business strategies and product developments. IT companies will have to provide solutions with Open Systems architectures that conform to emerging European standards, integrating different manufacturers' hardware and operating systems, and providing users with more information seamlessly across vast geographical areas, using highly flexible distributed relational database technology and fourth-generation languages.

## 7 Proprietary and Public Standards

*P.W.L. Morgan, IBM*

This chapter examines the case for a vendor adopting industry standards alongside or in place of their own, internally developed, technical specifications. It must be understood that industry standards give interchangeability of components and interworking at the expense of the optimality and maximal function provided by the vendor's own technical specifications. In the course of the discussion several topics related to the growth and use of standards are addressed.

In this way the chapter aims to make three significant points. First, all major reputable suppliers voluntarily, and positively, engage in the standards-making process for sound commercial reasons, and do so to achieve benefits which are not available by any other means. Second, it is important for the user and for government to understand the advantages and limitations of industry standards. Failure to do so leads to unrealistic expectations which will inhibit the rate of change and achievement in the Information Technology industry. Finally, if formal standardisation is to produce the benefits of which it is capable, then some drastic changes are necessary in the organisation of the standards-making process.

## 8 Why Open Systems – a management perspective

*C.V. Calder, AA*

By 1987 the Automobile Association (AA) had recognised the need for a new strategy within which to base its IT investments. Over the next year or so the Management Services group developed a forward-looking Open Systems strategy. This chapter examines that development process and the lessons which have been learnt.

Hundreds of management hours, plus the cost of external consultants were necessary to put the strategy together. It was not possible to formulate a reliable strategy until the business planning process was in place. Even then there was the need to disseminate the strategy and gain commitment from the general staff of the organisation. Attempting to change the culture of a management group and its staff is a non-trivial task.

The prize has, however, been worth the effort. The development process has acted as a catalyst to change Management Services' thinking and planning horizons. Every development or investment is a positive step towards the overall business goals.

## 9 Open Systems policies in the NHS

*P.J. Bishop, NHS*

This chapter describes Open Systems policies which are in place in the NHS and will give some examples of how they are being implemented in procuring IT products and services.

It briefly describes the NHS as an environment in which OS policies are important and the author describes the role and activities of that part of the NHS for which that author works – the NHS Management Board's Information Management Group – IMG, illustrating how the IMG is addressing Open Systems issues.

Finally this chapter discusses NHS policies that are in place for procuring products which conform to OSI Standards.

## 10 Implementation of a Value-added Network in an Open Systems market environment

*M. Anstee, Lloyds*

The objectives of this chapter are to:

convey the business requirements and objectives of the London Insurance Market Network (LIMNET);

identify the problems and opportunities of undertaking such a project in the light of the main participants being trade associations or membership clubs;

chronicle the selection of IBM as our Value-added Network supplier and subsequent developments.

Once this has been completed the author then investigates further the role of Value-added Networks and their relationship with Open Systems architectures, and whether they might become the major catalyst of industry standards.

## 11 Electronic Data Interchange: British Coal and the EDICT System

*W.L. Bedford, British Coal*

This chapter examines electronic data interchange (EDI) – the computer to computer electronic exchange of business information between business parties (and possibly intermediaries) in a structured format – in short, paper-less trading.

The business problem is to exchange formal documents such as orders, price lists and statements, without the delays and errors inherent in paper trading. Since 70% of computer input originates from another computer's output, direct transfer of data offers not only to solve these problems but also to reduce the cost of the trading process. This is illustrated by a case study of the introduction of EDI to British Coal's purchasing operations.

The advantages of EDI depend critically on the availability of appropriate standards for electronic business forms. Thus speedy migration to internatio-nal standard 9735 – EDI for Administration, Commerce and Transport – is necessary to achieve a truly global means of data interchange.

## 12   Planning for Information Resources Centres

*C. Lazou, ULCC*

For the last twenty years a small number of advanced research computer facilities have been established with the aim of providing to their researchers the most powerful computers available to assist in solving pressing scientific and engineering problems. In the USA, the Department of Energy Federal Laboratories, in Los Alamos, Lawrence Livermore, and recently University Supercomputing Centres funded by the National Science Foundation are typical examples. In Britain, National Centres like the University of London Computer Centre, the University of Manchester Regional Computer Centre and the Atlas Computer Centre at Rutherford fall into this category.

This chapter reviews the challenges which supercomputer centres face in helping geographically dispersed users to exploit a total information resource, from supercomputers, mainframes, departmental computers, to workstations and microcomputers.

## 13   Standards for scientific languages and library modules

*S. Hammarling, NAG*

This chapter is concerned with the standardization of languages for scientific computation, with particular reference to Fortran and Ada, and with the standardization of the specification of modules for basic scientific operations with particular reference to linear algebra.

Standardization of languages is vital in order to allow the ready transporta-tion of software between different machine environments, to enable the re-use of software components and to ensure a controlled, stable development of the facilities and features of languages for the scientific community.

With the advent of parallel processing and modern architectures, it is important that code remains efficient when ported between different machine environments, and this is one of the principal concerns in the standardization of basic library modules.

## 14 Development and application of software tools to verify standards

*A.T. Twigger, Unisoft*

The area of verification and validation is an increasingly wide sphere of activity which is gaining importance as demand for Open Systems across differing architectures grows. There has been a noticeable increase in interest in software quality assurance and in product and in product conformance over recent months with accreditation procedures being established, branding programs announced and standards efforts being completed. This chapter reviews the requirements for verification in the Open Systems marketplace and outlines some of the principles involved in producing software and providing services to meet these demands.

The context of this chapter is based on the author's experiences in generating software for operating system and for compiler verification. There are other areas in which verification is established, in particular networking, in which the same principles have been used to provide verification services.

# Part One

# Keynote Papers
# From Governmental Agencies

# 1

# GUIDELINES FOR AN INFORMATICS ARCHITECTURE

*W. de Backer*

*Director of Informatics Commission of the European Communities*

## Editor's Note

This paper is reprinted with permission from the booklet *Guidelines for an Informatics Architecture*, published by the Commission of the European Communities, (3rd edn), Brussels, 1988.

## INTRODUCTION

After decades of being locked into one or a few suppliers for all their computing needs, more and more corporate users in Europe, the United States and Japan are now switching to multi-vendor procurement policies based on standards. IT companies are responding to this user requirement by stepping up their own standardisation effort.

It is in the interest of all users to

> remain free to choose the best way to integrate new technology
> independently of the policy of individual manufacturers.

In addition, the European institutions have to cope with the complexity caused by different languages and partners in remote geographical locations. This turns an interest into a necessity, and dictates a high degree of flexibility in implementing those technologies.

More and more organisations understand why a vendor-independent strategy based on standards is feasible, economic and necessary.

1. It is feasible through an evolutionary path: proprietary interfaces can be phased out and replaced with standard ones.

2. It is economic because expensive interface adaptations can be eliminated and costly conversions avoided. Once users are no longer locked into vendors, competition in an open IT market brings prices down.

3. It is necessary if organisations are to communicate and interact effectively.

## Standards contribute to market growth

The limiting factor in market growth is not technological progress: customers are often offered more than they can use. Instead, it is the ability of users with different hardware and software to interact - this ability is only offered by standardisation.

This demonstrates that the market for standardised products is a growth market: standardisation has a multiplier effect. The more people can communicate and services can interact, the greater the volume of information they exchange - and the larger the IT market becomes.

## Industry and standard-making bodies must adapt to customer priorities

Industry and the standard-making bodies should listen to the requirements of customers for standards and understand the difficulties they have in implementing them; the risk of not doing so is to offer standards which cannot be sold, while other standards may be badly needed. In the standard-making process, this means missing windows of opportunity when these present themselves.

For these reasons, customers must co-ordinate their activities in formulating their standards requirements and make their voices heard so that industry will fulfil them. The CEC sees with satisfaction a growing number of customer associations taking the lead in standards implementation. The CEC as a customer wishes to encourage their efforts, contribute with professional information and experience and support proposals of common interest.

European users should lead the world in demanding standard products. If the IT industry in Europe supplies the solutions to such a receptive market, it can become competitive on a world-wide scale.

## An architecture is more than standards

Defining guidelines for an evolutionary architecture for the next decade is not an easy task. Most architectures have been designed by the computer manufacturers to match their present and future product ranges. Such architectures are, generally speaking, mutually incompatible even where standards are used.

A vendor-independent architecture can only be developed by the customer - but no single customer has the power to impose a given architectural design on industry. Consequently, such an architecture must emerge from the ongoing process of supply and demand.

This is the spirit in which these architectural guidelines have been prepared. They reflect neither specific customer needs nor particular design concepts; moreover, they take into account the availability of products on the market. This is an additional reason why the guidelines themselves are subject to constant review and correction.

## ARCHITECTURE

### Domain Structuring

User populations of autonomous organisations, such as private companies, government administrations and European institutions, have independent informatics management structures, here called **private domains.** (see figure 1.1). Private domains communicate via Public Communication Networks (PCN) and use services provided by **public domains**, which are managed by public telecommunication administrations (PTTs).

The distinction between public and private domains implies a distinction between inter- and intra-domain architectures. The first has to be determined by common agreement between all the domains concerned, whereas the management of each domain is autonomous in determining its intra-domain architecture. The definition of the intra-domain architecture, however, is significant if end-user interaction across domains is to be achieved.

A private domain is composed of **local domains** interconnected with a Computing Centre and Telecommunication Centre by a Private Domain Communication Network (DCN).

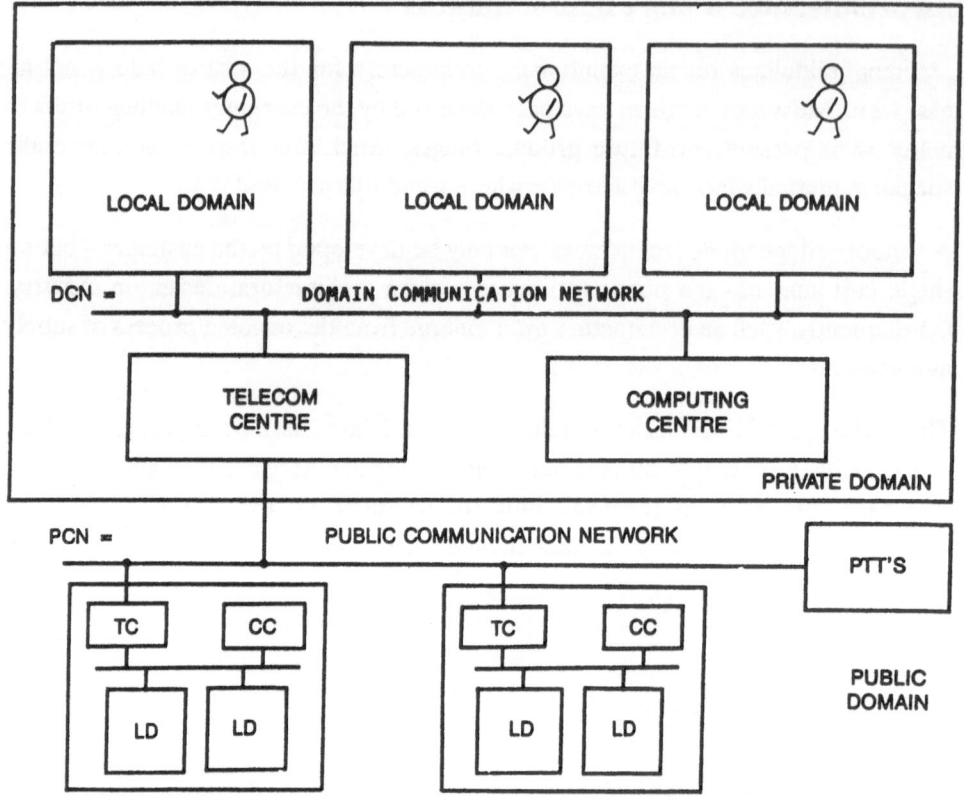

Figure 1.1: Public Domain.

A local domain is characterised by a close working relationship between its users and a common requirement for specific sets of services, thus justifying the cost of providing local support and management.

A local domain is equipped with a **local system** (LS), which includes local computers, personal computers, terminals, printers, a local communication network, management and user support. A local system (or departmental system) is thus an autonomous unit dedicated to the local domain.

A **comon system** (CS) of interconnected computers provides remote services to one or more local domains, the entire private domain or other private domains. Common systems are located only in computing centres and telecommunication centres.

The structuring of local domains does not apply to telephone networks. For further discussion of this matter, see section 3.2 in [1].

# Organising local domains

A local domain will generally coincide with an organisational unit such as a department at a single site. "Site" is not necessarily the same as "building". There may be more than one site within a building, or there may exist links between buildings to enable them to be treated as a unit.

A local domain should serve as large a user community as possible. If, however, a user community is divided geographically in such a way that it cannot be supported economically by a single local domain, it should be served by different local domains. Similarly, if a large user community consists of groups carrying out activities with little or no interaction, it should be served by different local domains.

The domain architecture as described above is intended for large and geographically spread organisations. Small organisations located in one building are advised to adopt an architecture similar to that of a single local domain. A gateway to the public networks could then contain a mini telecomunication centre.

Other deviations from the general model may occur when members of a local user community are not in the same office area but are separated by relatively large distances. If this is an exception, a pragmatic ad-hoc solution must be found without changing the architecture guidelines. There are cases, however, where user communities are spread over different countries (e.g. international committees), or even composed of mobile members (e.g. members of the European Parliament). Two solutions are then recommended.

1.  If administrative and/or secretarial support can be provided at some location for the community, this can be equipped with a local system providing a service access point. The distant workstations, preferably personal computers, are then connected by the public and private communication networks to the local system, from where all the services for the local community can be accessed.

2.  If such a service entry point cannot be provided, each user may then be equipped with a "single workstation local system", again based on a personal computer, or even, in some cases, simply with a terminal linked to services provided by the national PTTs (e.g. Videotex). In this solution, isolated autonomous users are considered as single-member domains.

## Distributed processing

One of the fundamental problems of an evolutionary architecture is to decide where to locate software and data on the computers in the network (see figure 1.2). In order to describe the problem more accurately, the following terminology is employed.

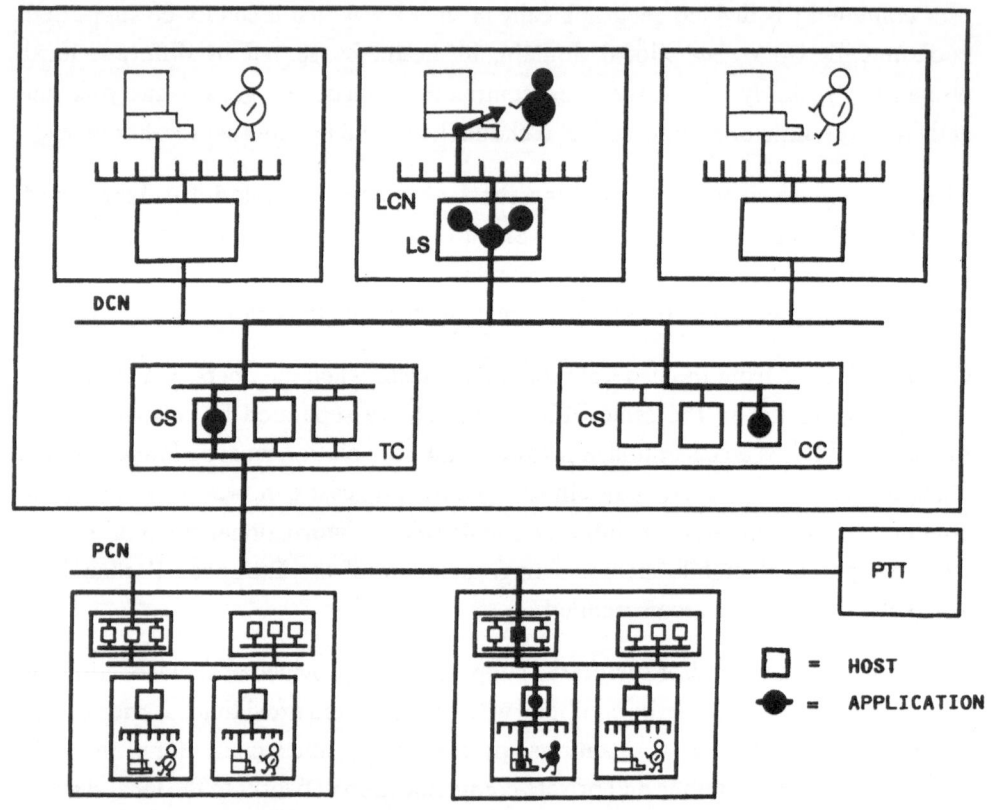

Figure 1.2: Distributed processing.

The **workstation** is either a terminal or a personal computer (including printer), although future integration of data, text, voice and image will lead to a single multi-function workstation providing access to all user services.

A **user service** is what users get at the workstation when they have logged into an application. Examples of user services are: access to a database, word processing, document management, electronic mail, and so on.

An **application** is a set of co-operating pieces of application software and data processed on the same host or on different hosts in the network.

A **host** is a computer with its operating system and the communication software necessary for its integration into the network. Interworking hosts not only process applications but also provide communication services such as interactive communication, file transfer and message handling.

A personal computer is, in line with the definitions above, both a workstation and a personal host.

The Open Systems Interconnection (OSI) reference model is fundamental for the architecture of hosts and networks but does not solve all the problems.

For applications to be processed by a given host, they must technically fit together. The more hosts that offer the same interface to applications, the easier it is to relocate application software on different hosts. Transportability of software is very important for an evolutionary architecture.

In order to define a distributed architecture one must decide

1.  how user services are provided up co-operating software and data on different hosts;

2.  how hosts are distributed in the network.

The decision rules are organisational (see above on domain structuring), economic, functional and technical. All of them change in the course of time. As a result of decreasing hardware costs, there is a shift from central to local processing, thus avoiding the chronic congestion of central hosts and networks. In general, the distribution of application software will follow the pattern in which data are distributed.

The natural location of application software and data is on a personal host (personal computer) when dedicated to a single user, on a local host when shared by the members of a local user community, or on a common host when shared by several local user communities, the whole private domain, and possible user communities outside the domain. However, for technical and economic reasons, they are often installed further upstream from the user. In the past, all applications were processed by the computing centre mainframes, and for large local databases, heavy batch processing and number crunching this is still economic today. Another example is where data for a single user are stored on a local host in order to implement data administration services.

It is technically possible, though undesirable, to locate common data downstream from their normal position and process them on local hosts. For reasons of responsibility, security and resource management, common user services must be provided only by the computing centres and the telecommunication centres.

## Applications architecture

Workstations, hosts and networks are merely the foundations that provide stability and support the applications. Computers and communications have become a commodity. The really difficult architectural problems start when the user organisation invests its own added value.

Most applications are based on software products requiring tailor-made development. This results in as many different architectures and user interfaces as there are applications. With their growing number, this becomes an unbearable situation both for the user and for those who have to maintain the applications.

Integration is the solution, but what is the framework to support this integration? The OSI reference model was not devised for this purpose. The so-called "client-service" model is a much more promising road to follow. Much will depend on whether this model will be followed by the designers of software products.

The problem is to assemble user services with commercially available software components such as those listed in Table 1.1.

**Table 1.1:** Commercially available software components

| | |
|---|---|
| Word processing | Formatted Database system |
| Spreadsheet | Data Dictionary |
| Data Entry | Thesaurus |
| Report Writer | Electronic Mail |
| Document Composition (DTP) | Integration software |
| Business Graphics | Statistical software |
| Geographical Information Software | Time management |
| Filling | Project management |
| Document Administration | Compilers/interpreters |
| Documentary Database | etc. |

Many software suppliers have already succeeded in integrating several components in the same products, although too often for a single host instead of a distributed host environment. The higher the level of integration, the more the internal archicture of the product becomes part of the overall architecture adopted by the user organisation. This is progress, but in the absence of standards it can also introduce a new type of captivity. For all these reasons, software products should be selected only if they

1. have an open architecture (easy to integrate other software components);

2. are transportable or at least are available on as many computers as possible;

3. provide a similar human interface (in the absence of standards, the best approach is to follow the most successful trends);

4. are designed for distributed processing, preferably following the client-service model.

A particularly difficult problem with architectural implications is multilingualism. International language coding tables must be outside the operating systems or application software and be processed as data.

User services are not independent from one another and also call on lower level supportive services. The structuring of application software and data covers more than distributed processing and also includes switching between user services, the content and location of databases and the information flow between them. The management of the private domain has to adopt its own architectural design in these cases.

Chapter 4 in [1] illustrates a possible approach.

## Standards

Commercial products are the building blocks of the architecture. They can only fit together when there is a 100% match between

1. all functions that have to interwork through the product interfaces;

2. the standards governing access to these functions.

The only solution to this problem is to employ functional standards or profiles that match the product interfaces. In the field of machine interaction,

CEN/CENELEC/CEPT, with the support of industry (SPAG), has taken the initiative in defining such profiles. The resulting ENV-EN standards must be fully complied with. These profiles are a direct application of ISO/CCITT basic standards. When ISO profiles are approved, they will supersede the EN profiles.

At present, functional standards have only been developed for the OSI model but they should be extended to all types of interaction between products (e.g. different software products on the same machine). We shall from now on use the term standardised products when the product interfaces conform with such standard profiles.

A customer pursuing a multi-vendor procurement policy will buy standardised products. Council Decision 87/95/EEC of December 1986 makes this an obligation for public procurement in the European Community. However, when such products are not available or have only a partial standards coverage, the customer will take what, in his judgement, is the best alternative available on the market. In association with other customers, he can handle deviations from standards through controlled procurement, put pressure on the standard making bodies and industry to get their priorities right and, if possible, introduce new standards proposals.

The introduction of standardised products is urgent, not only for economic reasons, but also because it will become more difficult the longer it is postponed. Computer applications (databases, wordprocessing ,electronic mail, document administration, etc.) are growing at a rate of 25% a year, which means that if we wait 10 years, the switch-over to standards will be much more difficult, if not impossible.

For this reason, one might expect a fast growing market for standardised products, but unfortunately this will not happen tomorrow. Today, many standards are still missing, especially in the upper layers of the OSI model. Those available now are not always option-free, or do not completely cover the functionality of product interfaces (standard profiles). When these problems are solved, paper standards must be turned into de-facto standards by industry developing and selling standardised products. But the customer, in line with his multi-vendor procurement policy, will require standardised products supplied with a conformance certificate from one of the official Conformance Test Centres now being set up in Europe. A conformance certificate will not necessarily guarantee interworking, however.

All this will take considerable time. In addition, we should not forget that the first deliveries of a new standardised product will not fit into a non-standard environment, that the customer cannot phase out equipment before the end of its economic lifetime (3 to 5 years), that industry must continue to sell the money-spinners in its non-standard product range and that the end-user wants stability and continuity in his applications. In short, an important market of fully standardised products will not emerge before ten years from now, and this is much too late for the reasons explained earlier.  Consequently, we must apply an implementation strategy long before the availability of fully standardised products. This is both possible and urgent. If we do not do this, the window of opportunity to a standardised market may be closed before we get there.

It is not possible to understand the priorities for standards and the market for standardised products without considering the customer trying to get away from a captive supplier-dependent architecture.  He can already, where standardised products are not yet available, implement interim solutions that are as vendor-independent as possible and integrate them into an evolutionary and carefully planned scenario in successive steps of about 5 years, aimed at closing the gap between proprietary architectures and a standard architecture.

The CEC has been successfully following such a scenario since 1980 and is now benefiting from the resulting cost improvements.

In the light of this experience, the following four subjects are of prime importance for standards work.

## Open System Interconnection (OSI)

The OSI model and related standards must be applied throughout the architecture and not just to bridges between proprietary architectures.  The major customers in the world, not only in Europe but also in the USA and Japan, are now putting their weight behind the implementation of OSI, to the extent of ignoring other standards.

The top priority for OSI should be remote access to databases, for which no satisfactory standards are available.  This is one of the important reasons why the information market has been so slow to take off.

## Applications architecture

The present lifetime of computers is 3 to 5 years, whereas applications survive for at least 15 years.  At the same time, applications software is migrating from central to local and personal hosts for economic reasons.  In order to protect investment in applications in an evolutionary environment, it is necessary to have a stable platform to build upon. In 1984, the CEC decided to adopt UNIX (or equivalent) for local systems as the best solution for this purpose.

Since then, a group of computer manufacturers with foresight (X/OPEN) has decided to co-operate in defining a standard interface between UNIX and applications software. This common applications environment will become more important than UNIX, as it will open up the software market.

Applications software will dominate the future, but the high development costs will not translate into profits unless the products can be sold for a world-wide computer base. This is why X/OPEN is so important, especially for Europe. Independent software vendors with good ideas will at last find an open market.

The CEC, as a customer, fully supports the adoption of the X/OPEN Portability Guide as an international standard, hopefully harmonised with the POSIX specifications in the USA.

The more the evolution of applications can be uncoupled from the evolution of hosts and networks, the easier it will be to speed up the integration process. But this makes all the more urgent the standards work on applications architecture, including the further development of the ECMA and ISO model for Distributed Office Applications (client-service model).

## Human interworking

In the decade to come, users will spend more and more time at their workstations with access to a growing number of user services, they will no longer accept

1.  software products employing a different terminology for the same functions;

2.  different languages and screen styles for each different application;

3.  different keys on the keyboard for the same function;

4.  different office procedures for work of a kind that is the same all over the world.

On the other hand, once users have been trained to master the complexity of a given user interface they will resist further changes. This shows the urgency of international standards for human interworking, but today their preparation has not advanced beyond a preliminary analysis of user requirements.

## Security

Security standards are necessary not only for their own sake but also because of their role in open systems interconnection and consequently the multi-vendor policy.

The implementation of security measures affects almost all components of the architecture — both hardware and software. In the absence of international standards, the IT industry follows the solutions developed by leading customers, in most cases national defence administrations. Even if these technical solutions are allowed in products for the private or public market, this remains a sensitive issue for both customers and suppliers in an open world market.

## REFERENCES

[1]   de Backer, W. (1988) *Guidelines for an Informatics Architecture* (3rd edn), Commission of the European Communities, Brussels, (ISBN 92-825-7945-X).

# 2

# UK GOVERNMENT PROGRAMMES TO ENCOURAGE OPEN SYSTEMS

*W. Greaves*
*IT Standards Unit, DTI*

## INTRODUCTION

The markets for many IT products and services are global. European manufacturers have suffered in the past from having a small home base in a fragmented European market. Progress towards a single market depends on the creation of a common set of standards and an opening up of public purchasing. These standards will enable IT equipment to be linked and work together, regardless of the make of equipment or its geographical location. Open Systems standards will thus create a free and open market for IT products and services, enabling manufacturers to compete on equal terms, and offering users the widest possible choice.

Government policy is to encourage the development of Open Systems standards and the products which conform to them. Most of the UK effort in the international IT standards arena has this objective. Many standards are reaching maturity and the DTI judges the time is now right to promote the concept of Open Systems within the UK marketplace to allow suppliers and users alike to take early advantage of the benefits which flow from them.

In consequence, in June 1988, the Secretary of State for DEI, Lord Young of Graffham, then announced a £12M, 3-year programme of awareness activities to transfer Open Systems technology into the marketplace, as an extension of the DTI's Enterprise Initiative.

This paper provides an insight into what the Open Systems Technology Transfer programme is, using Open Systems Interconnection (OSI) as a particular example.

## THE ENTERPRISE INITIATIVE

DTI, the Department for Enterprise, launched the Enterprise Initiative in January 1988. Quite simply, it is the biggest and most comprehensive self-help package ever offered to British business. It offers businesses both a valuable source of information and expert resources. Its aim is to put British business at the top by helping it develop in a number of ways. For example, it can put businesses in touch with experts in the fields of marketing, design, quality, manufacturing systems, business planning, financial and information systems. It can provide practical advice and assistance to those planning to export. It can help forge links with local universities and polytechnics, and it can help solve technical problems and give access to collaborative research projects.

Collaborative research and making best use of existing technology can be efficient ways of preparing businesses for future markets and competition. The Research and Technology Initiative, as part of the overall Enterprise Initiative, offers businesses the opportunity to undertake collaborative research, particularly with universities. It also creates awareness and understanding about existing technologies developed both at home and overseas and Open Systems technology is a case in point. It is one of three technology transfer programmes now being prepared, the others are in Advanced IT and Management Best Practice.

## OPEN SYSTEMS TECHNOLOGY TRANSFER

The overall objective behind the Open Systems Technology Transfer programme is to create awareness and understanding generally amongst IT users by giving them factual information about the different technologies which make up the concept of Open Systems and by providing solid evidence of its practicality in today's marketplace. More specifically, the aim is to stimulate a significant proportion of users to actually begin the process of transition to open systems within the next three years, i.e. by 1992. The time is therefore right for a concerted effort to drive home the importance of Open Systems and the aim is to spread general awareness among a large cross-section of the user population, then to deepen the education of a smaller but still sizeable number of companies, and finally to convince a core set of influential users that action is needed. Suppliers and consultancies, as important players in the game, will also be targeted.

Awareness can be achieved in a number of different ways, but the intention is to stimulate discussion by marketing Open Systems vigorously and then to highlight particular examples of how companies are planning, implementing and using Open Systems in their businesses to give them the competitive edge they are seeking. These examples will act as the signal for the beginning of the transfer of the technology into the marketplace and will, in turn, encourage others to take action.

The term **Open Systems** is used to embrace a number of different elements of IT which have the common objective of utilising internationally agreed standards, instead of the proprietary standards currently to be found in most IT products. DTI's programme of Open Systems Technology Transfer includes the different elements of Open Systems Interconnection (OSI), Software Quality, MAP/TOP (as specific user profiles of OSI), Common Applications Environment (especially POSIX), Security and Value Added Data Services (VADS). Each contributes to the concept of openness and will therefore be promoted in terms of the contribution it makes. To bring this about, it will be necessary to identify case studies, demonstrator projects, research programmes and centres of excellence relevant to each element.

OSI forms the backbone of the Open Systems concept and will therefore take the lion's share of the funding available for the whole programme. However, other than the fact that it is the largest element, the activities to be marketed under OSI are typical of those for the other elements also. For the purposes of this paper therefore, OSI is used as an example of the kind of activities appropriate to the whole programme.

## OPEN SYSTEMS INTERCONNECTION

### Case Studies:

Over the past two years, the DTI has been encouraging companies to undertake Opportunity Studies, partly funded by the Department, into the feasibility of adopting OSI progressively into their businesses. To date, thirty such studies have been completed and these have produced a wealth of information about the practicality of implementing OSI. (At the end of this paper are some general conclusions about the studies, together with a list of organisations which undertook them.) It is very important however, to transfer this information into the marketplace, so that other users can take advantage of the advice on offer. For the most part, the studies have concentrated on technical feasibility, but the key to success lies in getting business management on the side of the IT specialists and to narrow the gap between them in terms of their different levels of knowledge and different points of view. It is equally important therefore, to develop the business case for OSI. Technically, it can be shown that transition to OSI is feasible within a two to three year timescale, depending on what constraints are imposed on companies, but more research is necessary before all the business arguments are clearly defined and documented. Nevertheless, it is possible now to develop a number of case studies based on the Opportunity Studies and this is one of the first tasks. The case studies are aimed therefore, not only at technical management within companies, but also at senior business management and must be written in such a way as to appeal to senior (non-technical) management, i.e. in terms of the business needs of the companies, as well as the technical needs.

Production of the case studies is now well underway. Over the next two years a further twenty studies are planned which will concentrate on the business case rather than the technical issues and the Department would welcome proposals from industry for further research in this area.

## Demonstrator projects

Adopting Open Systems means change and change inevitably generates uncertainty. Industry and commerce rely heavily on IT to provide a satisfactory level of service and are realistic about its current commercial value. Adopting Open Systems may bring added value, but does it also bring added risk? Users needs a basis on which to judge. The early introduction therefore, of some user reference sites, seeking to implement Open Systems themselves, can enable the market to see its application in practice. From these, prospective users can see the practical implications, see how the risks can be reduced an examine the benefits. Such demonstrator sites give confidence to others that adopting Open Systems is feasible and worthwhile.

OSI Demonstrator projects are particularly valuable as sources of reference because they are based on users' real business requirements. They are not developed as research projects, but are implemented as live working systems. Other users are therefore able to observe the transition from existing systems relying heavily on proprietary standards, to those using products conforming fully to OSI standards. They can observe the technical and business implications of such a process. Of course, Demonstrator sites are accepting a risk that any difficulties encountered during the transition would receive the same publicity and attention as the successes. They are therefore to be congratulated both for their willingness to accept this responsibility and their foresight in wishing to take early advantage of the technology.

In early 1989 the Department identified four major OSI Demonstrators, each one concerned with a different application and involving the use of OSI products largely from different IT suppliers. Over the next three years, it is intended to encourage other users and suppliers to keep in close touch with the development of these projects and regular reports of progress will be provided. Over this period, the doors of the Demonstrator sites will be open for practical demonstrations of how OSI is meeting the demands of the users involved.

The first OSI Demonstrator was announced by Mr Eric Forth, the Parliamentary Under Secretary of State for DTI, in September 1988 and was officially opened by the Secretary of State, Lord Young, in the Spring of 1989. This is at Aston University and involves the installation of a high capacity campus-wide communications network serving the University, the Science Park and the Technology Transfer Centre. Students, academics and industrial partners will be able to access a range of innovative features such as applications of distance learning, information and document delivery, distributed electronic mail, teaching methods, communications technology and international communications (including satellite and a link to the Library of Congress, Washington).

## Guidelines

In addition to the case studies mentioned earlier, the Opportunity Studies have shown that it is possible to adopt a standard approach to such studies and this has led to the development of a Feasibility Study Methodology. The studies embodied in this methodology aim to determine the feasibility of adopting solutions, based on OSI standards, to business data communications problems.

Experience has shown that those carrying out a study of this kind will gain greater awareness of OSI in a general sense and, more importantly, a better understanding of the relevance of OSI in the context of their own organisation. Such studies are not intended to be all-embracing and do not replace the need for a well thought out data communications strategy.

The methodology defines a set of steps for undertaking the study, together with practical advice and guidelines on how best to complete each step. In this way, it helps users to concentrate on the content of the study, rather than the mechanics of carrying it out. The methodology has been designed primarily for those responsible for planning and managing the study, who will also often be responsible for planning or managing the IT and communications resources within their organisation. The study manager is not expected to be an expert in OSI standardisation however, although such expertise may be required from some source during the later stages of the study. The methodology is also useful to business managers in helping them appreciate the need for the study in the first place, although the practical guidelines contained in it are intended to help those undertaking the detailed work.

The methodology has been designed to be practicable for a wide range of organisations and business sectors. It is important to stress that it is a guide rather than a rigid set of rules and therefore lends itself to adaptation where necessary, although users should try to avoid diverging too far from the basic flow of the process, which has been proven in a number of DTI funded studies. A further document, which will eventually accompany the methodology, is a model to assist users in setting out the financial aspects of planning for OSI and convincing board-level decision makers of the benefits. The difficulty of this must not, however, be underestimated.

## Market Intelligence

Over the past two years and in conjunction with the CCTA, the DTI has published the results of two detailed surveys into the availability of OSI products. The most recent was published in May 1988 and is entitled *OSI Products: 2nd Report*. It is available from HMSO bookshops, priced £42.

The survey is a twenty-five part report on the current products and plans for OSI of 24 major IT suppliers. Both the DTI and CCTA are encouraged by the results and the trends in the development of OSI products. In general, suppliers are taking a positive approach to transition of their current proprietary communications products to OSI. Most have a significant set of currently available products and positive plans for further products in the near future. All suppliers have indicated a desire for common interpretations of, and conformance tests to, OSI standards, although some suppliers are not progressing as quickly towards this objective as users might wish to see.

The difficulty surrounding such surveys however, is that they take quite a while to complete and publish. On the other hand the OSI products scene is changing almost daily. Although the information contained in the reports is valuable, it would be far better if a way could be found of making it more timely. Accordingly research is being conducted into how to achieve this in the most cost-effective manner. When complete, it is hoped that users can be given up to date information about the OSI products which currently exist on the market, those which conform fully to the standards, having been subjected to independent conformance test suites, and those which have been demonstrated to interwork with similar products from different IT suppliers.

## Marketing strategy

OSI is a complex and wide-ranging subject. There are many facets to it, each of which is important in contributing to the whole picture. It is not easily understood, even by IT specialists. In the field of data communications there are a number of established architectures and protocols, and it is generally considered easier and safer for users to stick with tried and tested methods. In addition, business management does not generally understand IT, while communications presents even greater problems of familiarity. Thus, OSI faces considerable barriers before it can be accepted as part of the procurement plans of the typical user organisation. As awareness improves, however, it will become easier to break down the barriers of resistance and inertia, and the penetration of OSI in users organisations will increase.

The time is now right for a concerted effort to drive home the importance of OSI. Recognising this, a comprehensive dissemination and education programme is being planned, using the material developed from the above activities. The idea is to improve awareness in a consistent and market-oriented way, measuring progress by feedback as different stages are reached. Eventually, users will be equipped to decide how best to utilise OSI, and market forces be allowed to take over. By 1992 awareness should be at a very high level and that is when the really hard work will start! Everyone concerned with the future of IT in the UK is invited to consider how they can contribute to this enterprise.

# Appendix 2.1   OSI Opportunity Studies: A status report

*IT Standards Unit*
*Department of Trade and Industry*

## INTRODUCTION

Since 1976, the International Standards Organisation (ISO) has been developing a vendor-independent set of standards which will ultimately allow any computer, supplied by any manufacturer, to exchange information.

ISO developed the Open Systems Interconnection (OSI) Reference Model which specified an architecture or basic set of rules for defining the detailed standards which would later be produced. OSI grouped all interactions into seven distinct layers and specifications for standards exist in all seven layers. Although not all the standards are, as yet, stable and some still have to be properly defined, the stage has been reached where the majority are now sufficiently mature to encourage IT manufacturers to begin developing products which implement them.

## BACKGROUND

Historically, computer equipment manufacturers were not naturally inclined to adopt open systems because it could mean opening up their customer base to their competitors. They preferred instead to offer products based on proprietary standards which meant that users encountered considerable difficulty in exchanging information between dissimilar computers, sometimes even between the different ranges of the same manufacturer. Indeed, some major manufacturers have profitted from the lack of common standards by being able to set de facto standards. Not surprisingly, users tended to choose those manufacturers who had a large user base and a steady company background. Although smaller manufacturers have also adopted these proprietary standards, the degree of choice has been somewhat restricted for the user.

However, as communication of information within and between companies has become increasingly essential and technological advancements make possible new computer applications, the manufacturers now recognise that the ability to exchange information between different systems is commercially advantageous and, indeed, necessary if the market (and their sales) are to continue to grow.

With the growing demand from users for wider spread usage of computer applications, the requirements for systems which can interface across a number of functions and physical sites is becoming vital for business efficiency. The buying power of major and influential users has undoubtedly encouraged many suppliers to take action and develop ranges of OSI compatible products. As a result, virtually all the major manufacturers have now expressed their commitment to conforming to OSI standards and products are beginning to appear on the market. It is expected that within the next few years users will be able to freely build application systems based on them.

However, it should be recognised that the decision to adopt OSI standards is often complex and, as such, may be one which less forward thinking users are reluctant and apprehensive about tackling. Nevertheless, the benefits of OSI in improving business efficiency demand careful planning and, if user companies are to be prevented from missing the opportunity, they should now be considering OSI as an integral feature of their IT and Business Plans.

# OSI OPPORTUNITY STUDIES

## Basic Philosophy

To stimulate a greater awareness of the benefits of Open Systems, funding is available, mainly to organisations in the private sector, who wish to develop their OSI strategic thinking. Since its inception in September 1985, 28 organisations in both the public and private sectors have successfully applied for funds. These have been in the form of **Opportunity Studies,** of which the majority are feasibility studies into how OSI can be adopted to allow those organisations to progress smoothly from environments in which their incompatible computer systems prevent or hamper the ready exchange of information, to environments in which compatible systems positively encourage it. Typically Opportunity Studies take four to six months and, because external OSI consultants are usually necessary to offer expert advice, cost between £30,000 and £60,000. To encourage the take-up of OSI, the DTI offers up to 50% of the cost of the studies and the users contribution is usuallly met by using their own internal manpower resources which has the added benefit of allowing the users to build up their own OSI expertise - an essential ingredient when it comes to implementation.

## Approach

The Terms of Reference adopted depend entirely on the users' perception of their individual requirements, but the general approach ususally involves four distinct phases of study. The approach is strongly recommended for anybody wishing to undertake a similar exercise and is summarised as follows:

1   develop a Communications Architecture by identifying all the existing and proposed IT applications for the organisation and the need for communications and working between the systems they support;

2   by reference to the existing and planned OSI standards, identify which would be necessary to meet the requirements of the communications architecture and when those standards would be technically stable;

3   knowing what standards are needed and when they will be sufficiently stable to be useful, hold detailed discussions with selected IT suppliers and, together, identify what products will implement the standards, when they will become available and whether or not they will meet the requirements of the user;

4   taking all these factore into consideration and recognising the technical, financial and political constraints there are on the user for introducing changes, develop a transition strategy for the introduction of systems which conform to the OSI standards.

It must be appreciated that Opportunity Studies are essentially technical in nature and require genuine knowledge and expertise in the individual OSI standards. They also require commitment at the highest level from users themselves. If this is forthcoming, they offer a unique insight into the value which OSI can bring and a way forward in terms of strategic IT planning.

## General findings

It would be very satisfactory if a small number of studies such as this could point the way forward for the IT user community as a whole. Unfortunately, this is not the case since every organisation differs from any other and its requirements for inter working will therefore often be different. Even within this tiny sample of 28 studies the requirements for interworking covered elements of Local Area Networking, Wide Area Networking, office systems, factory automation, administrative systems, research systems, distributed data processing, file transfer, electronic mail and messaging. The requirements frequently invoked different standards and even different aspects of the same standards.

Consequently it isn't always possible to offer definitive advice, based on the results of these studies and expect it to hold true for all organisations operating in similar circumstances. Nevertheless there are a number of common threads which can and should be highlighted. These are as follows.

1   Transition to OSI is practical over a three to four year period. Some organisations may feel that this timescale is too long if they want to take early advantage of the benefits. If so, interworking between systems can often be achieved now by taking advantage of many interim solutions currently on the market, but a longer timescale is necessary for those systems which need to conform fully to the OSI standards. There are two good reasons for choosing the latter. The first is that some of the standards, together with the non-availability of conformance text suites, have not yet matured sufficiently to encourage the development of all the relevant OSI products. The second is that the internal constraints on some users may be such that they feel unwilling to abandon their current IT investment simply to introduce OSI, preferring instead to progress along a somewhat steadier transitional path.

A simple message arising from this therefore is that, even when the majority of OSI products are readily available, it might be prudent to plan the transition to OSI over a sensible timescale and to select interim solutions which offer a definite transition to fully open working.

2   Because of the number of different user requirements and circumstances, building OSI systems which cater for all eventualities, by implementing all the available standards, is unlikely to be a viable proposition. The sensible option is to use only those standards which meet users individual applications requirements. To achieve true interworking, it is necessary to use a profile of standards from all seven of the layers of the OSI Reference Model and different applications often require the use of different profiles. Thus, the Opportunity Studies identified functional profiles for each relevant application, which reflected the work being undertaken in Europe and worldwide to develop such profiles. Current examples are the Manufacturing Automated Profile (MAP), the Technical and Office Profile (TOP) and, of course, within Central Government, GOSIP for OSI

procurement. Over the next few years more profiles will undoubtedly emerge to satisfy industry sectoral OSI requirements.

In practice, depending on the number and type of IT applications required, any single user organisation will probably adopt a number of such OSI profiles for interworking purposes.

3   Although the concept of functional profiles provides most users with a solution for restricting the use of individual standards to a sensible number, it also poses a possible future problem. OSI is still an emerging technology and development work is continuing on certain standards. This is also true of standard functional profiles and any such profiles adopted now might be subject to change in the future. Until the OSI products can be tested for conformance to the full standards therefore, users must recognise that some profiles are transitory and they must be prepared to change as the standards themselves mature.

4   The general desire for fully open working, in itself, presents users with a possible dilemma. That is, whether or not to insist on fully open working between the systems directly under their own control. It is recognised that fully open working within the corporate boundaries of an organisation may not be essential. The absolute need for fully open interworking arises when organisations wish to exchange information with other independent organisations and therefore cross corporate boundaries. Although it makes sense to aim for fully open working both inside and outside such boundaries, for historical and political reasons, the OSI Reference Model contains legitimate standards which allow systems interworking that is not fully open and users must consciously recognise that, within their separate corporate entities, they have a choice to make. The strategic choice is how far fully open interworking should be extended into their individual systems and what future requirements they have for it. The technical choice concerns the use of connectionless or connection oriented standards within layers 3 and 4 of the OSI Reference Model.

## Some specific findings

Although Opportunity Studies are technically oriented, some of the users took the opportunity to begin to develop the business case for the strategic adoption of OSI. The following are extracts, selected from some of the reports and are representative of the conclusions arrived at:

1. **East Anglia Regional Health Authority**

(a) have computer systems from a number of manufacturers. The selection of computer equipment currently installed is not expected to limit the use of other manufacturer's equipment in the future.

(b) wish to maintain flexibility on the source of supplied systems and a competitive tendering policy. Such principles are difficult to adhere to if proprietary communications protocols are in use.

(c) have a wide range of communications requirements. Therefore a comprehensive set of complementary protocols are required, with clear migration and enhancement paths.

2. **GKN**

(a) Most units anticipate significant benefits in faster document turnround, timeliness, quicker responses, easing time-zone problems (for international traffic), improved productivity, cost saving, management of the business, competitive advantage and matching the capabilities of customers and suppliers.

(b) The cost of installing electronic mail facilities to X.400 standards may be partly justified by savings on conventional communications, but the decision is mainly not whether to implement, rather the timing of doing so.

(c) GKN should affirm its commitment to the principle of OSI and all GKN companies should actively promote OSI and the use of the appropriate standards with their major customers, trade suppliers and IT suppliers.

3. **Metropolitan Police Office**

(a) Assuming that the OSI architecture is adopted on all the IT systems under consideration, it is estimated that the upfront costs associated with OSI will amount to approximately £7M by the end of the decade. In comparison, if similar interworking facilities are implemented via gateways between proprietary architecture, the corresponding estimated upfront cost is £14M, incurred over the same period.

[NB Metropolitan Police Office wish to point out that the above figures are best guesses based on known conditions at the time of the study. They readily acknowledge that a full investment appraisal would be necessary before they could be justified. Nevertheless, they suspect that the order of magnitude is accurate.

(b)  In addition to substantial long-term cost savings, the principal benefits of adopting an OSI policy are:

(i)   vendor independence, with an emphasis on value for money selection;

(ii)  flexibility of expansion in directions not originally envisaged, which protects costly investment in IT systems and reduces the risk for system obsolescence;

(iii) increased effectiveness of personnel, who benefit from improved access to corporate data and from speedier electronic communication;

(iv)  direct cost savings accrued by multiple use of the terminal population and by sharing between IT systems of the general purpose corporate data communications network.

## CONCLUSION

A relatively brief article such as this cannot hope to do justice to the wealth of detail contained in the very comprehensive reports which are currently available about the OSI Opportunity Studies. All that can be offered here is a flavour of their contents, but the intention has been to show both sides of the current OSI scene. Further details of the individual reports may be obtained from the named contacts in the list at the end of this article.

One particular important feature which has and is still emerging from the studies is that OSI should not be taken lightly. Anyone wishing to adopt OSI but who doesn't plan for it properly is probably heading for difficulties. Because OSI is not proprietorial, users might be unwise to leave it to their suppliers of IT equipment to provide all the advice they need. Independent assistance can be sought from the IT Standards Unit, Department of Trade and Industry.

# Appendix 2.2   Strategic Planning for OSI

The following organisations have undertaken or are currently undertaking an OSI Opportunity Study. Further information on the type of study, its outcome and availability of reports can be obtained from the named contact in each case.

1. **Metropolitan Police Office**

   Jubilee House

   230-232 Putney Bridge Road

   London SW152PD

   Contact

   Mr M. Bloomfield

   081 785 8603

   *Title: Strategy for implementing OSI throughout the Met Police.*

2. **IT Standards Users Association**

   Centre Point

   103 New Oxford Street

   London WC1A IDU

   Contact

   Mr R. Walker

   071 379 7400

   *Title: Document Interchange.*

3. **British Gas**

   National Westminster House

   326 High Holborn

   London WC1V 7PT

   Contact

   Mr G. W. Bennett

   071 242 0789

   *Title: OSI-based network architecture for British Gas.*

4. **Berkshire County Council**

   Shire Hall

   Shirefield Park

   Reading RG2 9XB

   Contact

   Mr J. Peel

   0734 875444 ext 3910

   *Title: OSI in Royal Berkshire.*

5. **W H Smith**

   Greenbridge Road

   Swindon

   Wilts SN3 3LD

   Contact

   Mr T. Bazeley

   0793 616161

   *Title: OSI Strategy and Programme.*

**6. Loughborough University**   Contact
Computer Centre   Dr Anne Mumford
University of Technology   0509 222312
Loughborough LE11 3TU

*Title: The use of the Computer Graphics Metafile in the University Community.*

**7. GKN Group Management Services Ltd**   Contact
PO Box 18   Mr R. H. Reed
Cranford Street   021 565 2001
Smethwick Warley
West Midlands B66 2RS

*Title: GKN National and International Electronic Mail Feasibility Study.*

**8. Wandsworth Borough Council**   Contact
The Town Hall   Mr M. Rundle
Wandsworth High Street   081 871 6002
London SW18 2PU

*Title: Strategy to implement OSI within Wandsworth Borough Council.*

**9. Metier Management Systems Ltd**   Contact
3 Foundation Street   Mrs H. Thomson
Ipswich   0473 219661
Suffolk IP4 1BG

*Title: Proposal for the implementation of OSI Standards to fulfil Metier's long term communications requirement.*

**10. East Anglia Regional Health Authority**   Contact
Union Lane   Mr J. Barnes
Chesterton   0223 61212 ext 221
Cambridge CB4 1RF

*Title: Data Communications for Integrated Computer Facilities.*

**11. Northamptonshire County Council**   Contact
**Consortium**
Computer Unit   Mr R. P. Griffith
Northamptonshire CC   0604 256504
County Hall Northampton NN1 1DN

*Title : Development of an OSI strategy for Northants, Lincolnshire North Yorks and Oxfordshire Conty Councils.*

12. **Ordnance Survey**  Contact
    Romsey Road  Mr M. Hinds
    Maybush  0703 79 2586
    Southampton SO9 4DH
*Title: Development of an OSI Strategy.*

13. **Durham Constabulary**  Contact
    Police HQ Superintendent  W. Forrester
    Akley Heads  09138 64929 ext 2333
    Durham DH1 5TT

*Title: Using OSI to satisfy the demands for share/integrated access to Police, Local Government and Central Government Databases over large geographical areas but having full regard for the security aspects of such accesses.*

14. **Glasgow City Council**  Contact
    Computer Services Dept  Ms A. Kennedy
    112 Ingram Street  041 227 4589
    Glasgow G1 1ET
*Title: Housing Department Communications Review.*

15. **Thomas Bolton and Johnson Ltd**  Contact
    PO Box 1  Mr F. M. Fallows
    Froghall  0538 752241
    Stoke-on-Trent ST10 2HF
*Title: Investigation of potential for use of OSI in TB & J's Strategic Information Technology Plan.*

16. **Ener-Tech Electronics Ltd**  Contact
    25 Walkers Road  Mr S. Ballantyne
    North Moons Moat  0527 66592
    Redditch
    Worcs B98 9HE
*Title: detailed investigation of OSI in overall strategic Information and Integrated Manufacturing Technology Plan.*

17. **The Burton Group Plc**  Contact
    241 Oxford Street  Mr P.J. Webb
    London W1N 9DF  0532 494949 Ext 4468
*Title: The Burton Group Communications Strategic Review.*

18. **Essex County Council**
   Computer Dic
   County Hall
   Chelmsford
   Essex CM1 1JZ

Contact
Mr L. Graves
0245 267222 ext 2340

*Title: Essex CC/Police OSI Feasibility Study.*

19.    **Spillers Foods**
   New Malden House
   1 Blagdon Road
   New Malden
   Surrey KT3 4TB

Contact
Mr J. Child
081 949 6100

*Title: Corporate Data Communications Study.*

20 **Natural Environment Research Council**
   Holbrook House
   Station Road
   Swindon
   Wilts SN1 1DE

Contact
Mr J. Down
**0793 440101 ext 382**

*Title: Development of an OSI strategy for NERC.*

21. **British Standards Institute**
   2 Park Street
   London W1A 2BS

Contact
L. T. Robinson
071 629 9000 Ext 3079

*Title: Strategy for communications facilities at BSI to permit automated support facilities and migration of both to OSI.*

22. **Norfolk City Council**
   City Hall
   Norwich NR2 1NH

Contact
Ravl Sharma
0603 622233 Ext 2002

*Title: Development of OSI within Information Technology at Norwich City Council.*

23. **Manpower Services Commission**
   **(Training Agency)**
   Moorfoot
   Sheffield S1 4PQ

Contact

Paul Frost
GTN 2023 4548

*Title: Development and implementation of an OSI cluster controller with Virtual Terminal Protocol.*

**24. Glaxo Export Ltd**
63 Graham Street
London N1 8JZ

Contact
R. I. Worrall
071 253 1243

*Title: Study to evaluate OSI Communications Possibilities for for Glaxo Export Ltd.*

**25. British Airports Services**
Masefield House
Gatwick Airport
Gatwick RH6 0HZ

Contact
Matt Green
0293 595620

*Title: Data Communications Strategy Study.*

**26. Polytechnic of Central London**
309 Regent Street
London W1R 8AL

Contact
D. G. Roberts
071 486 5811

*Title: Study to evaluate the OSI communications possibilities for the Polytechnic of Central London*

**27. B.A.T. (UK & Export) Ltd**
Export House
Woking
Surrey GU21 1YB

Contact
K. Soden-Barton
04837 76111

*Title: Study to define an Open Data Communications Strategy.*

**28. Liverpool Health Authority**
District Headquarters
1 Myrtle Street
Liverpool L7 7DE

Contact
T. Armistead
051 709 9290 Ext 215

*Title: An investigation into use of OSI to support Healthcare Information Systems.*

**29. Polygram International Ltd**
30 Berkeley Square
London W1X 5HA

Contact
O. Kyte
071 493 8800

*Title: International Communications Standards Feasiblity Study and Development of Network Strategy.*

# 3

# TOWARDS A EUROPEAN GOSIP

*L. Caffrey,*

*Head of Open Systems Group, CCTA H. M. Treasury (UK)*

This paper sets out the role of CCTA and its involvement in OSI leading to the EPHOS development of the project; why the project is necessary, and what can be achieved through it.

## CCTA

The Central Computer and Telecommunications Agency (CCTA) is part of HM Treasury. Its business is to add value to Government Departments through the most efficient and effective use of IT. Central Government is the country's largest user of IT; investment in all these services in 1987/88 amounted to 1.8 billion. Some 18,500 staff are employed on installing and running computers, telecommunications and advanced office equipment to support public services and its internal administration. CCTA provides information and advice to Departments to assist them in the planning of their individual IT strategies. In addition, it acts as a focal point for suppliers and the IT trade, channelling user requirements within Departments back to the industry. In this way, it is able to exert considerable pressure on the market and influence product development.

CCTA's business divides roughly into four main areas. The most prominent of these is the procurement division based in Norwich which deals with the contracts for the majority of central Government IT purchases. In 1987/88 it placed orders totalling £335 million. Direct project support is offered to Departments on a consultancy type basis for individual procurements and new installations. CCTA manages many of the Government's operational services such as the Government Telephone Network (GTN) and more recently, the Government Data Network (GDN). Finally, and of most interest in this forum, CCTA develops longer term technical policy and strategic advice. It is from this area of work that support for EPHOS has evolved.

## OSI

CCTA has had a long-standing commitment to OSI. In October 1984 it issued a Statement of Intent informing Departments and the trade that we viewed OSI as the logical way forward for achieving commmunications and value for money in IT. This was followed in March 1986 by more detailed *Advice to Departments* setting out timescales for standards and expected availability of products.

Similar work has been taking place in Europe. In February of this year the EEC Decision 87/95/EEC made the specification of OSI and communications standard mandatory for public sector procurements within the EEC.

It was clear even before this decision took effect that purchasers of IT were in need of guidance on the use of standards within an OSI environment. CCTA experience had shown that although Departments were able to specify their needs in terms of size of task etc., in an Operational Requirement (OR), they did not have the specialist knowledge necessary to determine the relevance of particular standards.

CCTA has published a *Catalogue of Standards* which provides an annotated list of the most recent and frequently used standards. This also highlights which standards are covered by European legislation. The Catalogue assists a Department to identify the appropriate available standards, and make use of them in IT strategies and procurements. This type of Catalogue, however, does not provide a panacea to some issues that are of paramount importance to the purchaser.

CCTA in collaboration with the DTI has also published, through HMSO, an OSI Products Review (*OSI Products - 2nd Report*, ISBN 0 11 514632 6, price £42 net). This contains details on Government Policy and the current products and plans for OSI of twenty-four of the major IT suppliers.

By nature, international standards must try to be all things to all people. A base standards specification will contain a range of protocol subsets that are not necessary to all users. A choice of options within the standards will have to be made. The level of choice that faces the user at each procurement is extremely high. Similarly, there is no guarantee that every supplier will implement the same protocol subsets in their products. Indeed, given the variety available, it is less than likely.

This complexity presents the user with a number of issues. Firstly, he or she is unlikely to have the specialist skills needed to determine the applicability of standards options. Secondly, the availability and choice of products that conform to an individual's selection of protocols will be low while the cost remains relatively high. Finally, and most disturbing of all, while users select and manufacturers implement different subsets, OSI products will be compatible on paper but rarely interconnect in practice.

# GOSIP

CCTA recognised that Departments were in need of firm guidelines if they were to purchase IT systems capable of interworking. The only way to do this was to refine the standards and tailor them to the needs of a particular environment; in this case, civil administration. In other words to adopt a limited number of options or a **narrow stack** selection from OSI standards. In August 1986 CCTA set up the GOSIP (Govenment Open Systems Interconnection Profile) Project and placed an open invitation with the IT industry - suppliers and test houses - as well as to Departments to join us. All were extremely supportive of the project and contributed a great deal of resource in terms of technical expertise and information on product development. The objectives of the project were threefold:

1. to facilitate procurement and acceptance testing of communications-based products;

2. to ensure that different and separately procured Departmental systems can interwork to an assured level of functionality;

3. to provide a clear specification to manufacturers on which to base strategic product development.

GOSIP carefully tracked the work of other organistions producing similar profiles (MAP, TOP etc), the functional standards being developed by CEN/CENELEC and CEPT in Europe, and agreements by the NBS and COS in the USA. This was crucial if there was to be any degree of interworking between systems adhering to different profiles and helpful in minimising the scale of the implementation task for suppliers. Hence, we aimed in GOSIP towards practical OSI products available for procurement at the earliest opportunity.

GOSIP was published as Version 3.0 in January 1988. In terms of a finished product, it comprises a set of documentation: A Management Summary and Introduction, intended for senior management, to establish objectives and set the project into context; the Specification, intended for the technically minded, suppliers or test houses who will need the level of detail contained in this document; and a

Procurement Handbook for project officers within Departments who will wish to avoid any specialist detail except where it is absolutely necessary. This is unique, similar documentation tends to ignore the needs of the non-specialist procurer.

Today, GOSIP V3.0 covers those areas of OSI for which clear Departmental requirements are known, and where products will be available. Figure 3.1 illustrates the areas that are fully covered and those areas (security, directory and management services) where because of the status of international standards, we have only been able to provide interim advice.

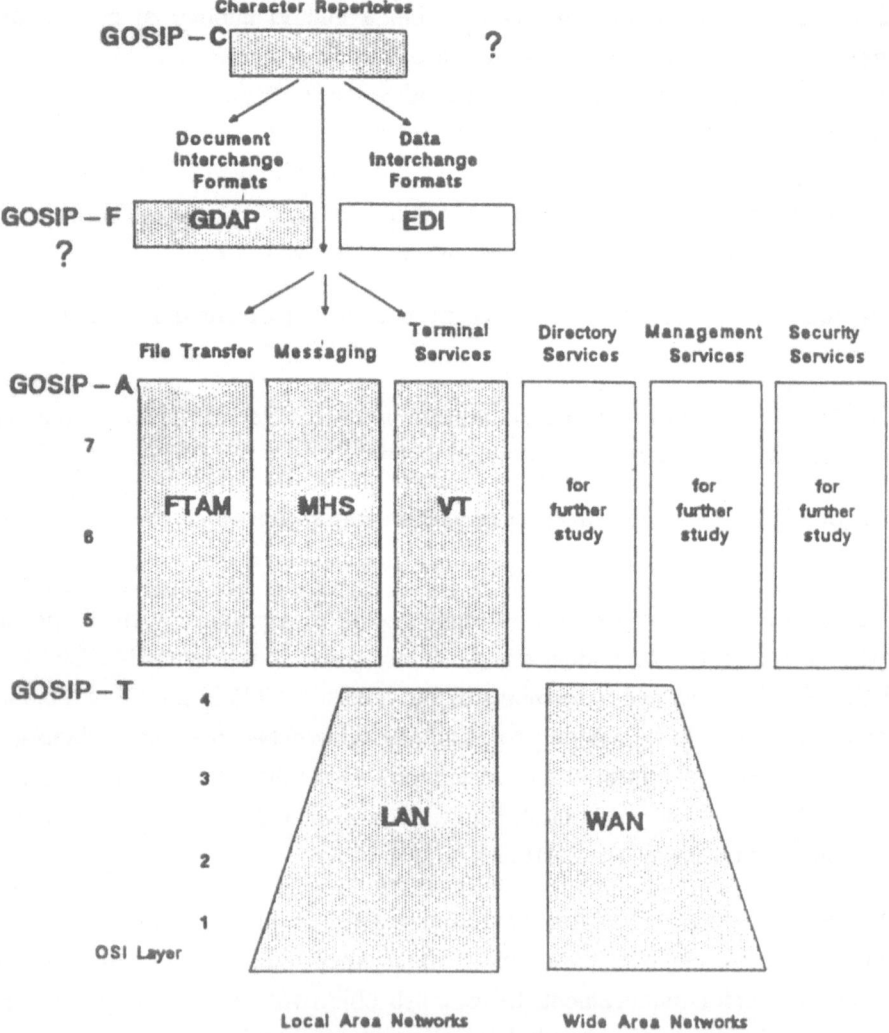

Figure 3.1: GOSIP - UK Government OSI Profile.

# IMPACT OF GOSIP

The impact of GOSIP Project has been enormous. Following the UK initiative, the US has created a profile also called GOSIP which is aimed at the US administration. This is to become mandatory for a number of US Departments including the Department of Defense. Other Governments, recognising the value of GOSIP, are developing profiles of their own. These include Canada, Sweden, Singapore, Korea, Australia and Norway.

In early 1988, CCTA was approached by the French administration to discuss the possibility of translating GOSIP. Following similar discussions with the German authorities the three administrations concluded that a better approach would be to develop a European profile based on the experiences of the GOSIP team. A project involving the UK, France and Germany (with the EEC attending meetings as observers) was set up in June 1988. The project is currently known as EPHOS, the European Procurement Handbook for Open Systems.

# EPHOS

Following detailed discussions between the three partners and the EEC it was agreed that there was a need to avert the problems which would arise from each member state preparing a functional profile to meet its own OSI procurement needs. Multiple profiles provide the user with choice he may be ill prepared to make and suppliers with the complications and costs of supporting multiple products, which may be incompatible. The proposal to produce a procurement hand-book suitable for use within all three administrations and meeting the legislative requirements of 87/95/EEC was adopted.

Following discussions within the EEC, including SOGITS (Senior Officials Group for Information Technology Systems) and PPSC (Public Procurement Sector Committee), the outline project plan was endorsed. Discussions are now proceeding with the EEC on funding for the project.

EPHOS will commence with a base provided by UK GOSIP and is to utilise ISO standards and CCITT Recommendations together with European profiles. Technical decisions will be based on the work of OSI Workshops, such as EWOS (European Workshop for Open Systems). The project will be conducted in an open manner with all EEC member states and EFTA kept informed of progress.

## OBJECTIVES

EPHOS will provide for public purchasers a simplified reference to functional profiles on OSI. It will contain documentation which is acceptable to European Administrations as the reference material required for procurement purposes to satisfy 87/95/EEC. It would thus supercede other national guidance in the same area of standardisation.

The Handbook is for use by those officials who specify what is required from their IT suppliers. It will explain in procurement rather than technical language how to use and specify OSI standards. Guidance will be given on:

1.  which specifications need to be referenced given a layman's under- standing of the requirement;

2.  how to reference those specifications;

3.  appropriate conformance testing and problems of interworking.


Project organisation will be through a number of Working Groups each tackling a functional area of work. The first version of EPHOS will be restricted to FTAM, MHS and X.25 based transport. Security and EDI will also be considered during phase 1. The Working Groups are under the direct control of a Project Manager from CCTA who reports to a Project Board. Each administration has a seat on the Board. The EEC will assist as observers. The documentation will be under a single editor and subject to independent quality assurance. The project is expected to take 300 man weeks and intends to publish late 1989.


## CONCLUSION

EPHOS is therefore entirely a user initiative for harmonisation of OSI procurement within the EEC. It will provide guidelines for both purchasers and vendors and limits the risk of different countries producing sub-profiles incompatible with proven products. The EPHOS profile is well positioned to meet the requirements of 87/95/EEC taking as its base the GOSIP documentation, GOSIP itself being the most comprehensive set of guidance on Open Systems for public sector procurement agencies in the world. The work will support and underpin the guidelines published by the EEC for an information architecture. The success of

GOSIP has proved that functional standards for OSI such as those proposed for EPHOS can work in practice. Such products are being provided today in ever increasing numbers.

# Part Two

# Vendor Views of Standards and the European Market

# OPEN SYSTEMS INTERCONNECTION: GAINING A FOOTHOLD IN EUROPE THROUGH STANDARDS

*R. A. Matthews,*

*Director Network Systems ICL*

## INTRODUCTION

OSI is an architecture - a means of achieving communication between computers, terminals and systems whatever their source or their manufacturer. It is, in a sense, a grand design for IT communications, expressed in terms of a seven layer reference model.

The OSI seven layer model and the means of implementing it is frequently seen as a technical subject, dealing exclusively with data communications. However, the reason for introducing OSI and the overriding importance of open systems is related to business needs and not pure technicality.

The most important consideration is that OSI consists of a set of genuinely international standards. This means that they are under public change control and that they do not favour any particular nation, continent, supplier or user in the market place.

In this context, they will be the key to the fully competitive European market which will exist after 1992.

The combination of a broad open architecture supported by open standards, which are under public change control, is also the key to achieving a **European commonwealth** of multi-vendor networked solutions which will be competitive in both European and world-wide markets.

The whole rationale for using Open System Interconnection standards is the obvious need to bring together the existing European base of multi-vendor systems and to provide an easy mechanism for the growth of new and more sophisticated solutions.

Business today is more and more concerned about the control, management and exploitation of information. It could be said that only two conditions are required for an enterprise to exist: shared goals and shared information. This, in itself, is not new. The new element is the ability to ensure, through information technology, that the information which is important to an enterprise can be shared both in terms of geography and function.

Most information is, in one way or another, held in computers and this leads naturally to the need for computers to communicate with each other.

In addition, business is increasingly transacted electronically between enterprises and this will increase as European companies regroup to meet the challenges of an open Europe. The consortia will depend more and more on the exchange of information between computers to carry out transactions with suppliers, customers, partners, and other third parties. Business in the European and international markets will thrive on such exchanges of information both within organisations and between organisations.

To make such exchanges feasible we require a common means of communicating, and we can only achieve that common language through the adoption of standards which are independent of both suppliers and markets. Standards which have the complete backing of the totality of the industry on both the supply and demand side.

Although standards are commonplace in other markets, industries and areas of life, it is worth reminding ourselves of the important benefits which derive from the adoption of public standards in information technology and, in particular, in the area of communication between systems.

Firstly, open standards create a stable environment in which users can confidently plan for the future. In other words, they can plan in a context which is free from change to a particular supplier's offerings, on the basis of whim or predatory intentions.

Secondly, the user acquires a freedom of choice which has, hitherto, been denied. This is particularly important as we enter an era in which IT becomes all pervasive - where no supplier can be best at everything and where it is a major benefit to customers to be able to choose the system or solution which best meets his needs, in the sure knowledge that he can integrate it into a total system involving solutions from other suppliers.

Thirdly, both suppliers and users can concentrate the investment of their resources in areas which are of the highest value.  Thus, IT becomes a common basis for competitive differentiation in Europe and other world markets.

Next, having invested in the best solution for the job, the customer knows that investment will not suddenly become obsolete through progress made by his supplier in the area of proprietary communications development.

Last, and probably the most important of all, the wide adoption of OSI standards will, undoubtedly, enlarge the market and make it more accessible to more specialist suppliers with the overall effect of making the European market more competitive with spin off into world markets.

These are all very compelling reasons for supporting the move to OSI standards for Europe.

The support for the Open Systems is widespread and has brought suppliers together to work for these common ends. We have arrived at a position which is a great deal healthier than many sceptics in the market would have you believe.  We are now at the watershed between the push of technology, representing the initiatives taken by the supply side of the market, and the pull of the market itself, which is expressed in procurement specifications which specify OSI standards and profiles.

The Open Systems movement has acquired an unstoppable momentum and the next two or three years will see enormous strides in terms of the take up by users in the market-place, and it will certainly dominate the European IT market.

ICL is totally committed to Open Standards which are seen to be an essential part of the continuing development of both  European and  global markets.

As a European based company, we see public international standards  making a major contribution towards the realisation of an open European market which is important to all suppliers and users in terms of market accessibility and critical mass.

More specifically, our commitment to Open Systems is reflected in the fact that OSI represents the architectural basis of ICL's Networked Product Line (NPL), which is the integral set of products designed to meet the common needs of all our customers.

As such, OSI is the infrastructure and the common basis for the industry solutions which differentiate ICL in the market place.  Through OSI, we can minimise our spend in the common infrastructure for interconnection and basic interworking and place an increasing part of our development investment in creating industry solutions, the area which is of the highest value to our customers.

ICL is not alone in recognising these opportunities and a considerable effort has been invested in the creation of the base OSI standards.  The major breakthrough in the OSI standardisation process has taken place over the last four to five years, during which the manufacturers and users have focussed on selected sets of option free standards for specific practical requirements.  The use of these **Functional standards** or **profiles** will guarantee interoperability of conforming products.  It is this breakthrough which has created the opportunities for market expansion in Europe through OSI and the background and the initiatives which drove the functional standardisation thrust are described below.

## THE ROLE OF FUNCTIONAL STANDARDS

### Reducing the Choices - Minimising the Options

The template for Open Systems Interconnection, known as the **Seven Layer Architectural Model** (figure 4.1), was designed to bring order to the IT standardisation process.  All the standards for Open Systems Interconnection are targeted to fit into this model.  It was created by the International Standards Organisation (ISO), which is the principal standardisation authority in the IT field.  The model has also been adopted by the International Telephone and Telegraph Consultative Committee (CCITT), which is the equivalent principal authority for telecommunications standards.

The principles are simple:  each layer represents a key function in the overall system operation and it carries a reasonably descriptive title, which outlines the  basic function of that layer. **Base standards** are created for each layer to perform that designated function.

The base standards for each layer cover a wide range of technologies and applications and they include sophisticated operational characteristics with various classes, options and parameters.  This introduces the risk of incompatibility if different options are selected. This risk can be removed by limiting the options and relating their choice to  actual user requirements.

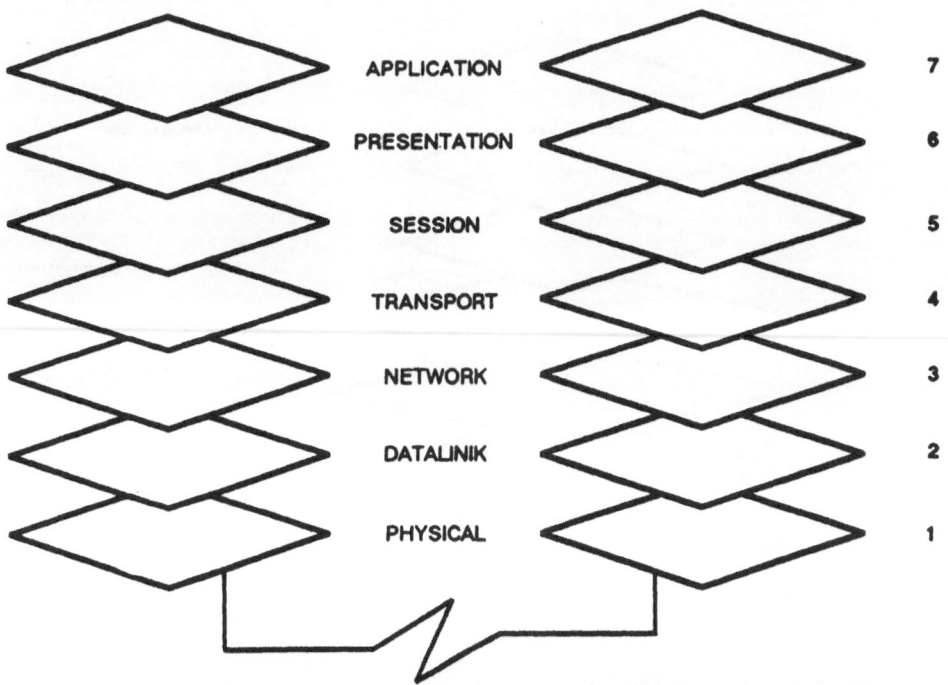

Figure 4.1: ISO Seven Layer Model.

This requirement has triggered initiatives to select a manageable number of practical standards which can be fitted together like building blocks to construct any networked solution. This process has become known as **functional standardisation** and the standards sets which are created are referred to as **profiles.**

Functional standards do not involve the creation of new base standards. They simply combine existing OSI base standards to deliver a well defined function to the user. The profiles are not completely option free, but great care is taken to include only those options which can be chosen freely, without disturbing the basic interworking with systems which exclude them.

## Separating the Functions - Interconnection and Application Profiles

The concepts behind functional standardisation can be better understood if the **seven layer** model is regarded as a **two function** model (figure 4.2).

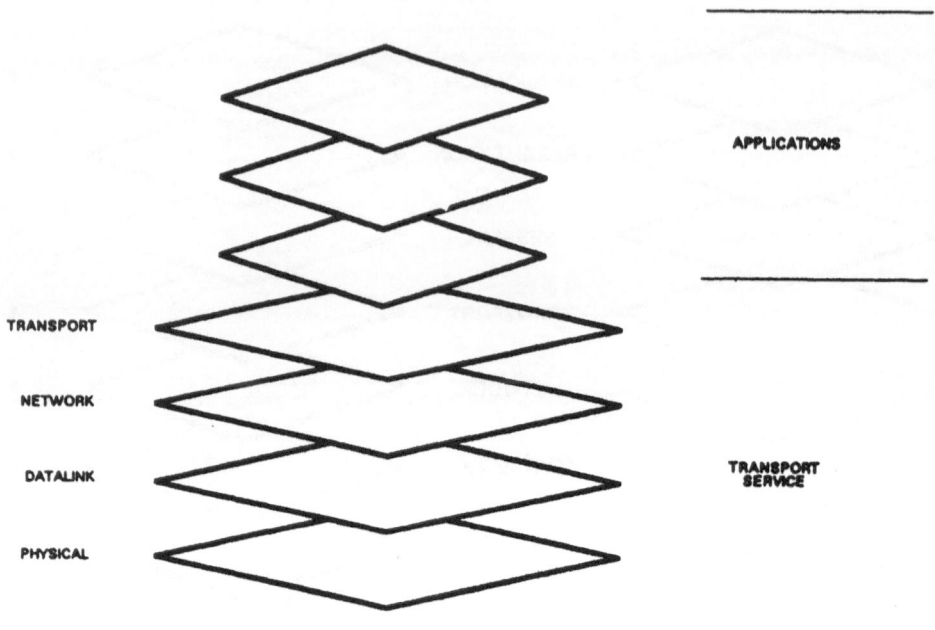

Figure 4.2: Two Function Model.

Layers 1 through 4 are the networking or interconnection layers which are commonly referred to as the **transport function**. Layers 5 through 7 are the application layers, which interwork through the transport function.

The Transport Layer forms a neat dividing line between interconnection and interworking. It quarantines the upper three layers from the underlying network, allowing standard applications to run over any kind of local, wide area or integrated services digital network (figure 4.3).

The division at the transport layer allows a simple concept of the model to be evolved around the interconnection and interworking functions. Figure 4.4 illustrates the concept of being able to select, independently, any interconnection profile (layers 1 to 4) to support any application profile (layers 5 to 7) and this simplifies OSI migration planning as will be seen later.

The services element in figure 4.4 refers to management, security and directory services, which are being merged into the structure by the standards organisations as the base standards mature.

The profiles are in two sets - Interconnection and Applications.

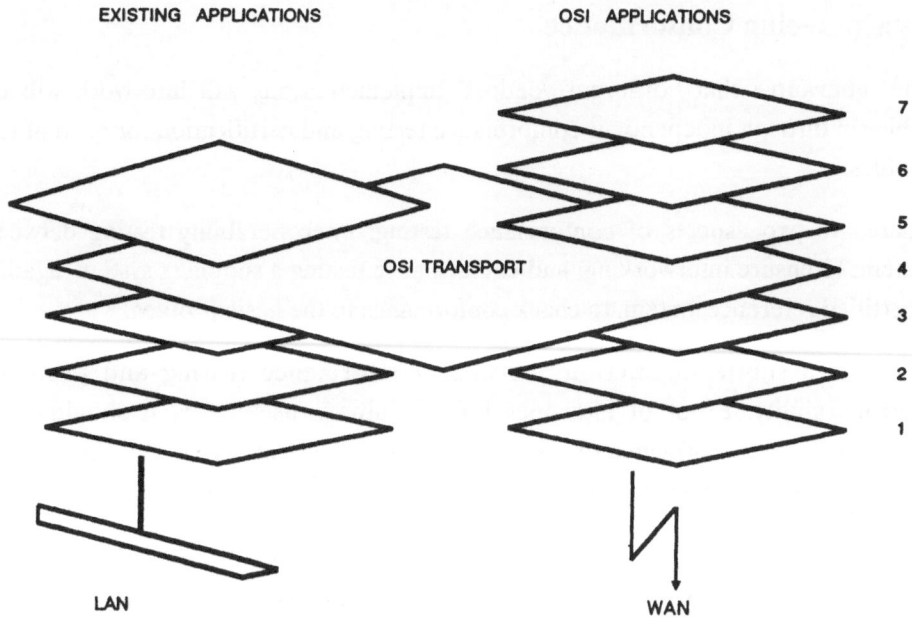

Figure 4.3: The Transport Layer as a dividing line between the applications and the network.

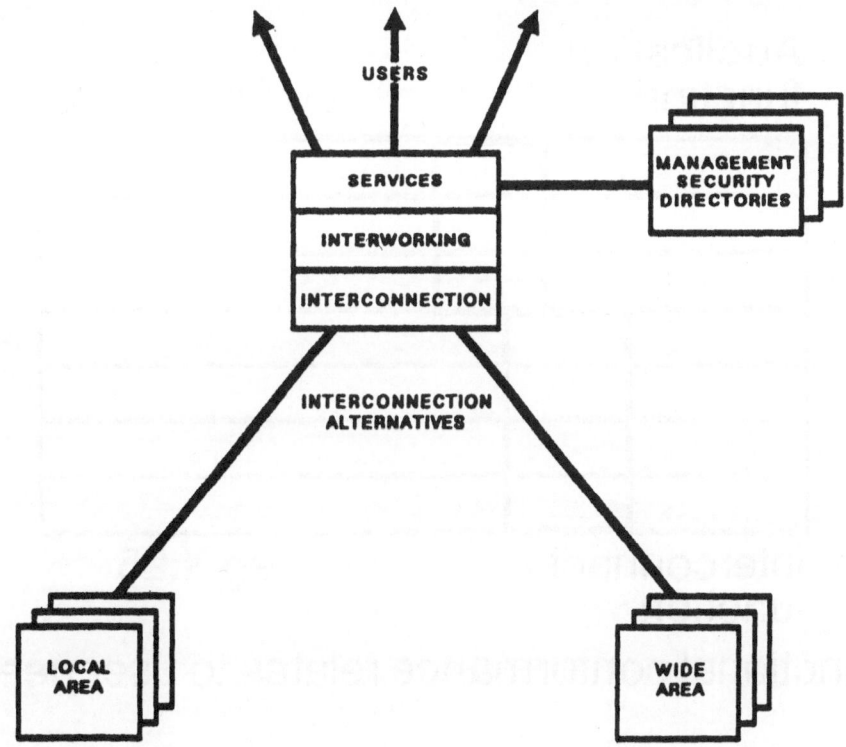

Figure 4.4: Interconnection and Applications.

### Guaranteeing Conformance

The **guarantee** that different vendors' implementations will interwork will be achieved through independent conformance testing and certification for each of the profiles.

There are two aspects of conformance testing: interoperability testing between systems to ensure interworking; and conformance testing a suppliers system against a certified reference system, to check conformance to the basic profiles.

There is a subtle distinction between conformance testing and proof of interoperability. Proof of interoperability is always useful, but it should be a formality if the conformance to profiles has already been checked. For this reason, the effort is being concentrated on creating tests for profile conformance.

Interconnection and application profiles are tested separately (figure 4.5) and the test houses tend to specialise in one or other of these areas.

## CONFORMANCE – THE USER VIEW

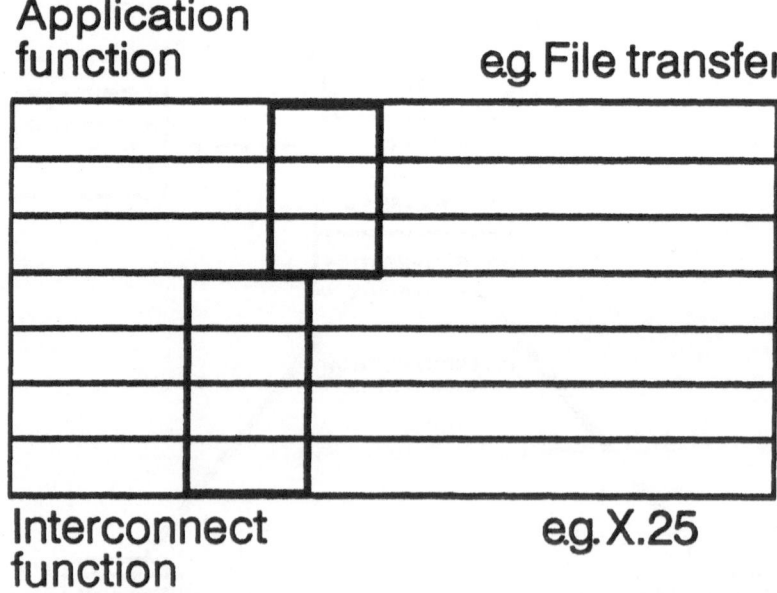

Application function

eg. File transfer

Interconnect function

eg. X.25

Functional conformance relates to user needs

Figure 4.5: Interconnection and application conformance.

The requirements which must be satisfied for conformance to each profile are specified as a set of **protocol implementation conformance statements** (PICS - figure 4.6). The supplier must declare conformance to these PICS when submitting his system for testing.

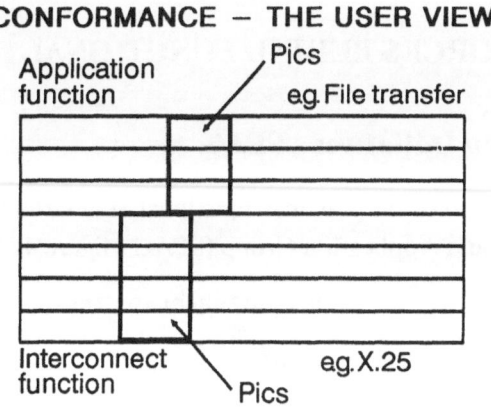

CONFORMANCE – THE USER VIEW

Functional conformance relates to user needs

Figure 4.6: The PICS (protocol implementation conformance statements).

Several organisations world-wide (figure 4.7) are addressing the above areas and interchanging their testing tools. The goal is a single, agreed set of tests and tools to ensure that a pass by any accredited testing agency guarantees world-wide conformance. The Commission of the European Communities (CEC) has already

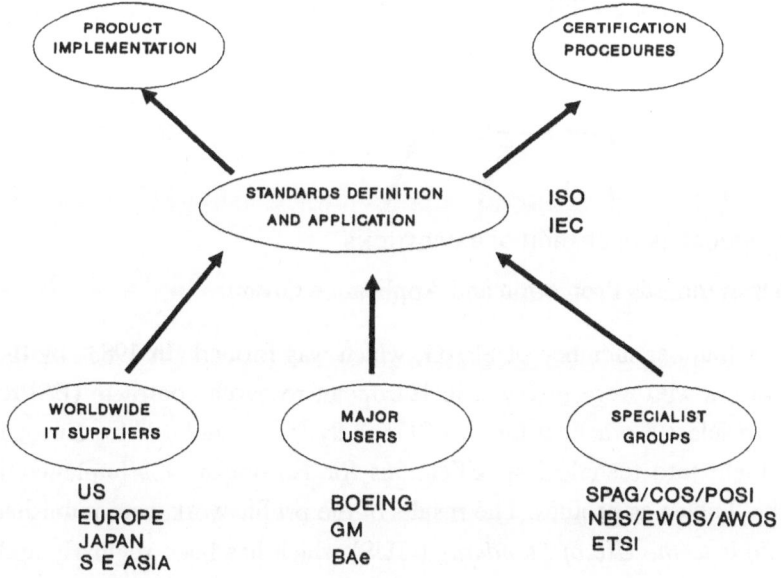

Figure 4.7: Worldwide movement for Open Systems.

issued directives which call for certification by any of the accredited test houses within Europe to be accepted by the other member nations. This is another important step towards a fully open and competitive European market.

## THE DRIVING FORCES BEHIND FUNCTIONAL STANDARDS

### The First European Initiatives - SPAG

The key driving force towards practical functional standards in Europe was the Standards Promotion and Application Group (SPAG - figure 4.8).

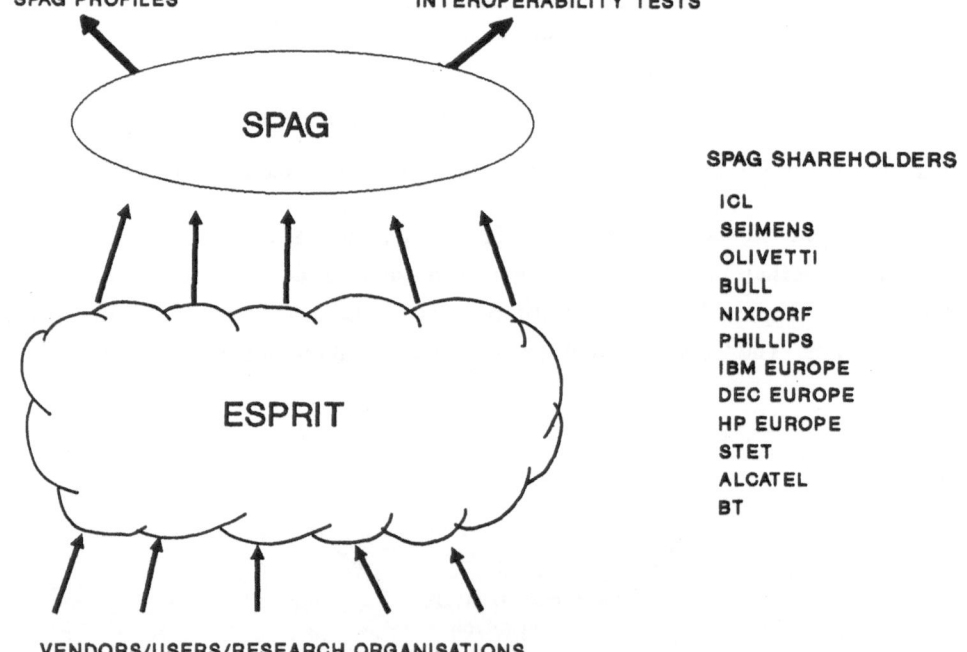

Figure 4.8: Standards Promotion and Application Group.

ICL was a founder member of SPAG, which was formed in 1983 by the major manufacturers who were involved in European research contracts (ESPRIT). Its goal was to select a practical family of Open Systems standards for Europe and to develop them into technical specifications for European OSI implementations - later to be known as profiles. The results of the profile work were published in the *SPAG Guide to the Use of Standards* (GUS) which has been regularly updated to include new profiles, based on new standards as they mature.

SPAG was reorganised and registered as SPAG Services SA in 1986 and has expanded its operation to include interoperability testing, with emphasis on OSI application profiles and MAP testing.

The SPAG initiatives stimulated the other major functional standards activities, both inside and outside Europe, and these will be described as the evolutionary story unfolds.

## The First USA Initiatives - MAP/TOP

The first functional standards initiatives in the USA were taken by General Motors and Boeing who made separate decisions to create standards for shop floor automation and technical office systems respectively. These two initiatives were soon related and are now universally known as Manufacturing Automation Protocols (MAP) and Technical and Office Protocols (TOP). The MAP and TOP profiles are regarded as a complementary family.

The USA MAP/TOP User Group has retained its autonomy, with GM and Boeing taking the executive lead and the Society of Manufacturing Engineers (SME) and the Industrial Technology Institute (ITI) providing the secretariat and support funding. There is currently a combined MAP/TOP User Group Steering Committee with individual MAP and TOP Executive Committees to control the MAP and TOP specifications. The technical work is carried out by Task Force Working Groups, some of which are run by the USA National Bureau of Standards as joint MAP/TOP/NBS - OSI Implementers Workshops. A joint MAP/TOP Test Committee is working on a conformance testing programme.

The MAP/TOP organisation is evolving. The effect on the European scene and the establishment of a world-wide Federation is discussed later.

## Acceleration in Europe - CEN/CENELEC/CEPT

The SPAG work became so successful that, in 1984, the Commission of the European Communities (CEC) asked them to join the Information Technology Advisory Expert Group on Standards (ITAEGS) to advise on the production of European functional standards. Other members were the Joint European Standards Institutions (CEN/CENELEC), and the Conference of European Telecommunication Administrations (CEPT).

This brought the European national standards making bodies, administrations, manufacturers and users into the functional standards making arena and soon led to the development of a series of European pre-standards, some of which are in the process of becoming full European standards. In many cases the original SPAG profiles formed the basis for the work.

All public sector procurement after 1992 is expected to be based on these European standard profiles and it is critically important that they should be harmonised with the profiles which are being developed world-wide. This harmonisation process is described later.

## Action by Manufacturers in the USA - COS

The success of the SPAG initiatives in Europe were recognised in the USA and, in 1985, twenty major USA computer and communication companies met to address computer communication, interconnection and interoperability problems. The outcome was the formation of the Corporation for Open Systems (COS - figure 4.9),

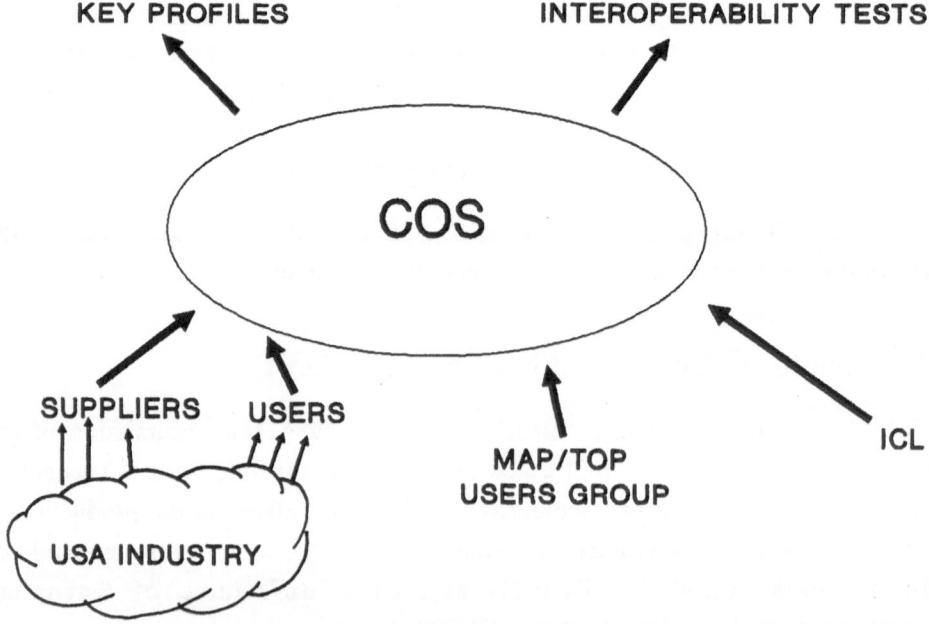

Figure 4.9: Corporation for Open Systems.

an organisation which now consists of more than 65 top industry suppliers and users, working together to achieve a common set of Open System goals. The MAP/TOP Users Group has joined COS to help the harmonisation process.

The main objectives of COS are to select a small number of existing Open Systems standards that will support user applications in many industries, to endorse specifications for implementing them and to provide conformance testing for products and services.

Like SPAG, COS does not create standards but simply endorses profiles of existing Open Systems standards. They normally reference National Bureau of Standards (NBS) agreements for both the endorsed profiles and the implementation details.

A longer term COS goal is to provide full interoperability testing of products with a view to providing problem-free interworking.

ICL were invited to join COS in 1986 in recognition of their role in sponsoring functional standardisation in Europe and is still the only European based supplier with COS membership. ICL has been given a seat on the COS Board and is actively promoting the harmonisation of activities between COS, SPAG and other world-wide functional standards groups.

## Japanese Functional Standards Activity - POSI

The initiatives of SPAG and COS were recognised in Japan and six companies plus Nippon Telephone and Telegraph (NTT) formed the Promoting Conference for OSI (POSI - figure 4.10) in November 1985 to promote OSI standards and to co-operate with other international groups having the same objective.

POSI makes the policy on the selection of OSI profiles and on the development of functional standards among the member corporations but overall control is exercised by the Interoperability Technology Association for Information Processing (INTAP) of the Japanese Trade Ministry (MITI) who actually create the OSI functional standards, devise conformance tests and provide OSI demonstrations.

At this point, the importance of standardising Functional Profiles had reached world-wide acceptance, but the actual work was still fragmented with no formal harmonisation process.

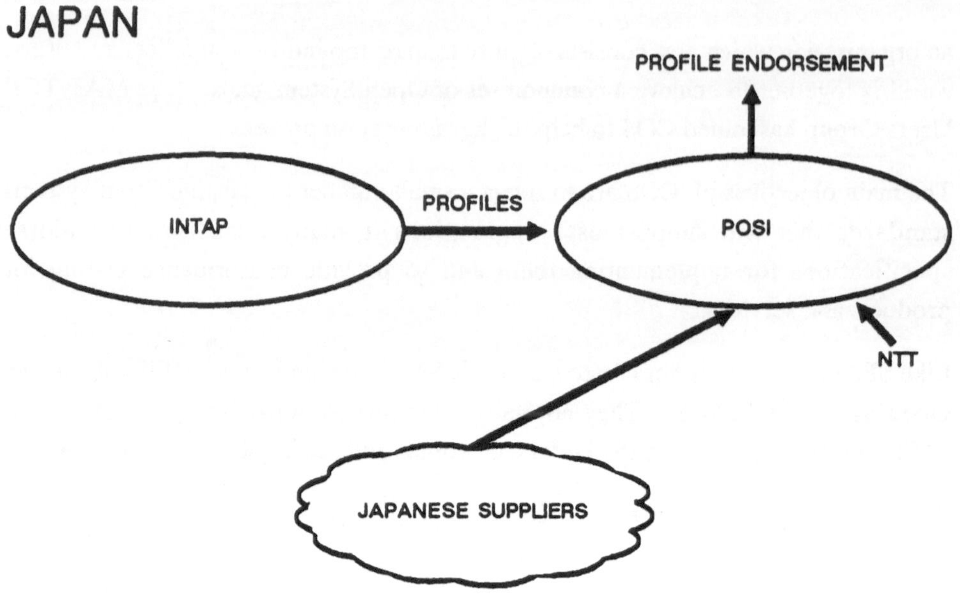

# JAPAN

PROFILE ENDORSEMENT

INTAP

PROFILES →

POSI

NTT

JAPANESE SUPPLIERS

Figure 4.10: Promoting Conferance for OSI.

## European Standardisation Goes Open - EWOS

Late in 1987, the CEC widened the scope of the European functional standardisation activity by chartering two new organisations to take over both the IT standards profiling work, which was being progressed by CEN/CENELEC

# OPEN EUROPE

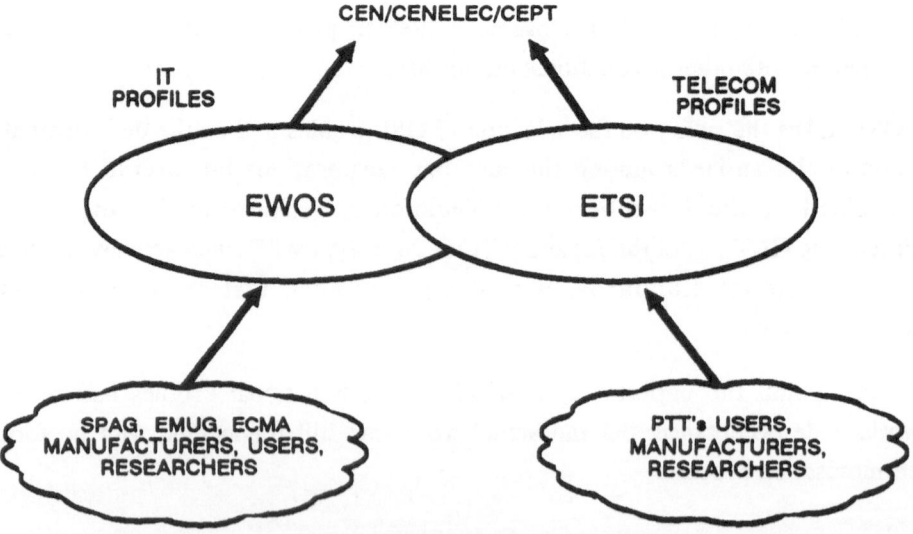

CEN/CENELEC/CEPT

IT PROFILES

TELECOM PROFILES

EWOS

ETSI

SPAG, EMUG, ECMA MANUFACTURERS, USERS, RESEARCHERS

PTT's USERS, MANUFACTURERS, RESEARCHERS

Figure 4.11: European Workshop on Open Systems.

committees, and the telecommunications standards work, which was being progressed within the CEPT. The two organisations are the European Workshop on Open Systems (EWOS - figure 4.11) and the European Telecommunications Standards Institute (ETSI). Both organisations became fully operational during 1988.

The associations involved in the formation of EWOS were CEN, CENELEC, SPAG, OSITOP, EMUG, ECMA, RARE and COSINE. EWOS is now an open forum for all those experts who are willing to contribute, and has become the new focal point in Europe for the development of OSI profiles and conformance testing specifications. It has its own management and budget, but remains within the overall structure of the Joint European Standards Institute (CEN/CENELEC). All the founding organisations will participate on equal terms in the management.

EWOS is managed by a Steering Committee with representatives from the founding members, headed by the EWOS Director. The development of the required profiles will be handled by Expert Groups (EGs) with a Technical Assembly (TA) to approve technical decisions. Each profile activity will be run as a development project with short term targets. The Technical Assembly is open to representatives from any organisation that is willing to contribute at Expert Group level. Any expert who is willing to contribute can participate in the EWOS Expert Groups.

This has created an open environment with simple rules which will attract more contributors to participate in profile development.

The documents produced by EWOS will focus on international harmonisation and will be targeted towards rapid standardisation both inside and outside Europe.

The other CEC initiative, which transfers the telecommunications aspects of functional standardisation from the CEPT to the new European Telecommunications Standards Institution (ETSI), opens up the work still further. Membership of ETSI is open to PTTs, manufacturers, users and research institutions. ETSI has its own management and budget and, like EWOS, it feeds its output through CEN/CENELEC/CEPT for pan-European endorsement.

European functional standardisation is now truly open and targeted towards the acceleration of international harmonisation. The generation of common telecommunications standards by ETSI is bound to simplify the rules for attachment to telecommunication services by the administrations across the CEC member nations.

## MAP/TOP Goes International - World-Wide Federation

The immense interest in obtaining practical standards in the manufacturing environment, which began in the USA MAP/TOP organisation, stimulated the formation of other MAP/TOP user groups world-wide, figure 4.12.

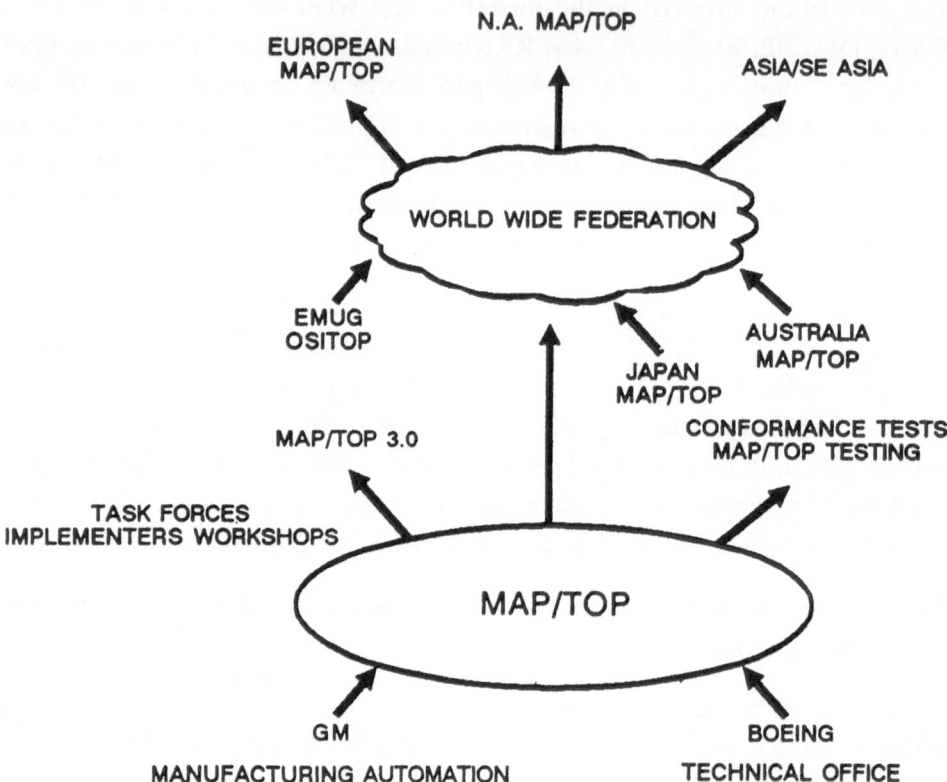

Figure 4.12: MAP/TOP.

The key expansion in Europe took place in 1986 with the formation of EMUG and OSITOP. These have taken an active role in supporting European needs during the development of MAP/TOP.

Other organisations world-wide are the Japan MAP Users Group and the Australian MAP/TOP Interest Group. The USA MAP/TOP User Group organised a world-wide Confederation of MAP/TOP User Groups to act as a focus for these regional activities with SME providing the Secretariat. Participation was focused into four regions: North America, Europe, Asia and Australia/SE Asia.

The USA MAP/TOP administration will change by the end of 1988 with the creation of a new (North American) MAP/TOP Organisation with its own full time staff and all its funding derived from an enlarged membership. The mission is being strengthened to include the promotion of the use of the MAP/TOP profiles to increase the overall market and force down prices.

MAP/TOP has used the ISO base standards and it is no accident that their results are closely aligned to the profiles which have been developed by the other key players. They are actively participating in the international profile harmonisation work as will be seen later.

## The Regional Activities Merge - The Feeders Forum

In 1986 SPAG and COS established a new working agreement to progress common goals. The senior technical committees (the SPAG Technical Committee and the COS Architecture Committee) held several joint meetings.

The close co-operation soon led to the formalisation of the relationship with both groups endorsing the COS and SPAG Harmonising Agreement. Under this Agreement SPAG and COS committed to harmonise profiles, test tools and test suites with the intention of promoting international Open Systems Interconnection and Integrated Services Digital Network (ISDN) testing services.

In 1987, the relationship between the international players was widened to include collaboration with POSI and MAP/TOP.

To promote the harmonisation of these national and regional OSI initiatives, the title Feeders Forum was given to the collaboration between SPAG, COS, POSI and MAP/TOP . They now continue their work together in this wider sphere with an ongoing programme of management and technical meetings.

The results were dramatic and representatives visited each others' technical committees and working groups to discuss alignment. Senior level contacts were made between the Feeders Forum and the Executive Board of ISO (now linked with the IEC in a joint IT Standards group) and liaison paths were established which became the key to international profile standardisation under the ISO/IEC umbrella.

An OSI Asian and Oceanian Workshop (AOWS) has been created, along the same lines as EWOS and the NBS Workshop. It will include participants from Japan,

Korea, China, Thailand, Singapore, India, Australia, New Zealand, and Indonesia. This workshop will take its place alongside EWOS and the NBS Workshop in the ISO/IEC functional standards harmonisation process.

## The ISO/IEC Umbrella - International Standards Profiles

International harmonisation of the profiles is critically important to both manufacturers and users. If a commonwealth of interworking OSI products is to be realised, we must employ internationally standardised profiles rather than local variants. This is important in both European and world-wide markets.

ISO/IEC entered the functional standardisation process in 1986 to fulfil this need. The ISO/IEC Joint Technical Committee 1 (JTC 1) have formed a Special Group on Functional Standardisation (SGFS) in which both ISO/IEC members, Feeders Forum groups and regional workshops can participate.

ISO/IEC will produce **International Standardised Profiles** (ISPs). Draft ISPs will be produced by members of the Feeders Forum, harmonised and endorsed by the

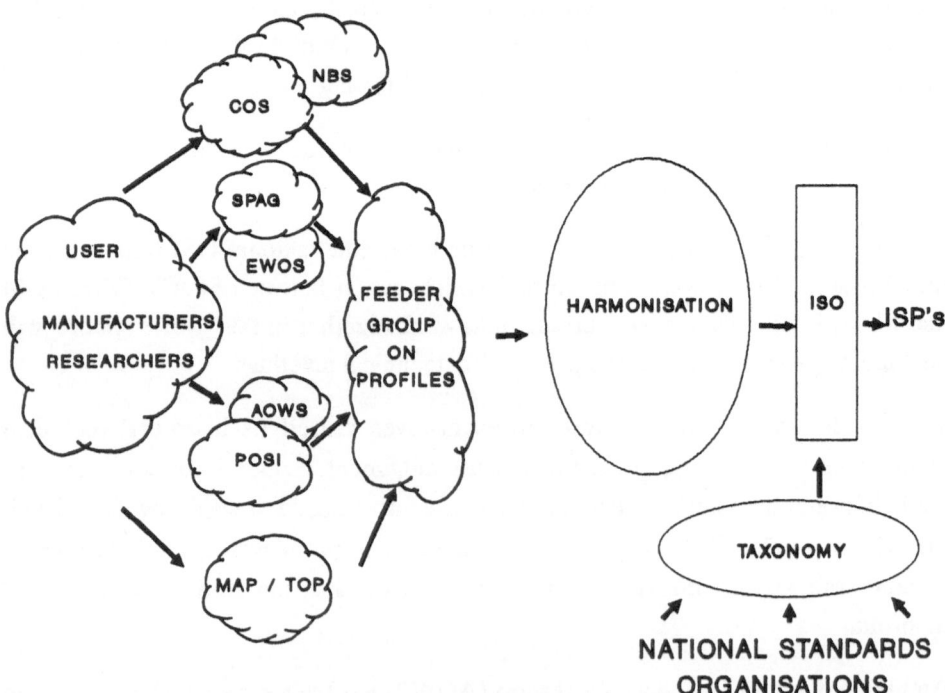

Figure 4.13: ISO/IEC harmonisation.

regional workshops (EWOS, NBS Workshop, AOWS), and then forwarded to ISO/IEC JTC1 (figure 4.13). Harmonised drafts will be subjected to a rapid check and ballot process within ISO/IEC and then published as ISPs.

The enthusiasm and energy behind the activity will ensure its success and will further stimulate the world markets into adopting OSI for procurement.

## THE KEY PROFILES

Activity within both EWOS and ISO/IEC has focused on the creation of a set of standard interconnection profiles for local area network and wide area packet network operation and the key application profiles for file transfer and message handling.

The key ISO/IEC profiles, which will become the first set of international standardised profiles (ISPs), are summarised in figure 4.14. They are:

FTAM
(SPAG)

| | UNSTRUCTURED FILES | | | | |
|---|---|---|---|---|---|
| | | | | | |
| | SESSION | | | | |
| CLASS 4 | | CLASS 0, 2, 4 | | CLASS 4 | |
| INTERNET  X.25 PACKET | | X.25 PACKET | | INTERNET | |
| LAPB | | LAPB | | LLCI | |
| | | | | CSMA/CD | |

| WAN | WAN | LAN |
|---|---|---|
| (COS) | (POSI) | (MAP/TOP) |

Figure 4.14: Responsibilities for the profiles.

1. LAN - Class 4 transport running over connection-less Internet protocol, LLC1 and CSMA/CD - MAP/TOP have the responsibility to progress;

2. WAN - Class 4 transport running over connection-less Internet protocol, and the X.25 packet protocol - COS have the responsibility to progress;

3. WAN - Class 0, 2 and 4 transport running over CCITT X.25 packet protocol - POSI have the responsibility to progress;

4.  FTAM  - Simple File Transfer for unstructured file hierarchies - SPAG has the responsibility for progressing the FTAM profile for this class of file transfer through to the ISP level.

Work on message handling profiles (X.400) was originated by the International Telephone and Telegraph Committee (CCITT), who published separate profiles, using ISO base standards.  These profiles have been progressed regionally within SPAG, CEN/CENELEC/CEPT and NBS workshops and a good degree of harmonisation has been achieved. Additions to embrace the enhancements in the latest 1988 CCITT Recommendations, will be progressed quickly to ISP level.


## THE SUPPORT FOR FUNCTIONAL STANDARDS


### Manufacturers, Users and Governments

The creation of sets of functional standards has been a major breakthrough and most major organisations are now  basing their future procurement strategies on conforming OSI profiles.

Of course, this was the original intention of the MAP/TOP initiatives but they were initially regarded as rather specialised in application.  However, the early work of SPAG and the subsequent international collaboration on the creation of general purpose OSI profile sets has changed all that and users can select the appropriate profile for their requirements.

MAP/TOP has, in turn, generalised its set of profiles, known as MAP/TOP 3.0 and this standard is sweeping into the manufacturing and technical office environments. The general purpose lower layer profiles exactly match first ISPs for interconnection and the only environment specific one is a LAN standard for the actual manufacturing shop floor.

CNMA (Communications Network for Manufacturing Applications) is a European ESPRIT collaborative group on MAP/TOP application and testing, which embraces British Aerospace, ICL, Seimens and many other European users and manufacturers. They have  established a CNMA Conformance Testing group to create MAP/TOP testing tools.

UK GOSIP (Government OSI Profile - figure 4.15) has declared support for OSI by publishing a set of profiles, which will be specified in future UK Government procurement tenders. This is referenced V.3.0. Once again, all the general purpose profiles are aligned with the first set of target ISPs.

## GOSIP

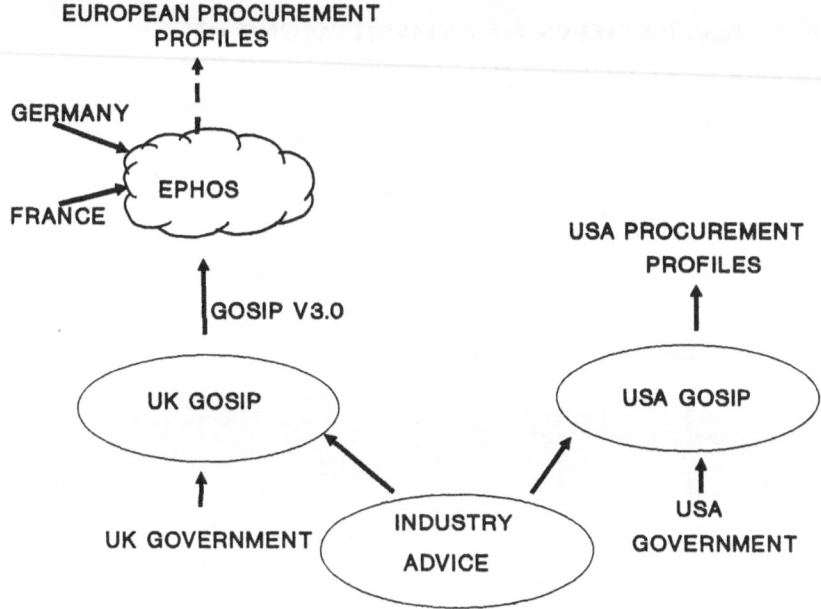

Figure 4.15: Government OSI Profile.

The USA also has a GOSIP organisation which is specifying the OSI profiles which will be used in US Government procurement tenders. UK and USA GOSIP are maintaining links to ensure that their procurement profiles are harmonised.

The work of UK GOSIP is already being considered by France, Germany and Sweden for their own procurement tenders, and other European nations are bound to follow. The UK is providing focus and leadership and there is every likelihood that we will soon see a EuroGOSIP procurement standard. All this has been made much easier to agree because of the European standards pedigree of the profiles involved. We have recently noted the first meeting between the European, USA and Japanese government procurement agencies (IPSIT) to explore common ground and this is bound to lead to world-wide agreements.

Underlying all this we have the clear CEC directive that all procurement within the open Europe beyond 1992 will be based on OSI standards.

## DEMONSTRATIONS OF COMMITMENT BY MANUFACTURERS AND USERS

### ENE88i

The June 1988 ENE88i (figure 4.16) exhibition in Baltimore was a clear demonstration of manufacturers' commitment to the functional standards. Many impressive practical applications of the MAP/TOP profiles were demonstrated in simulated manufacturing environments.

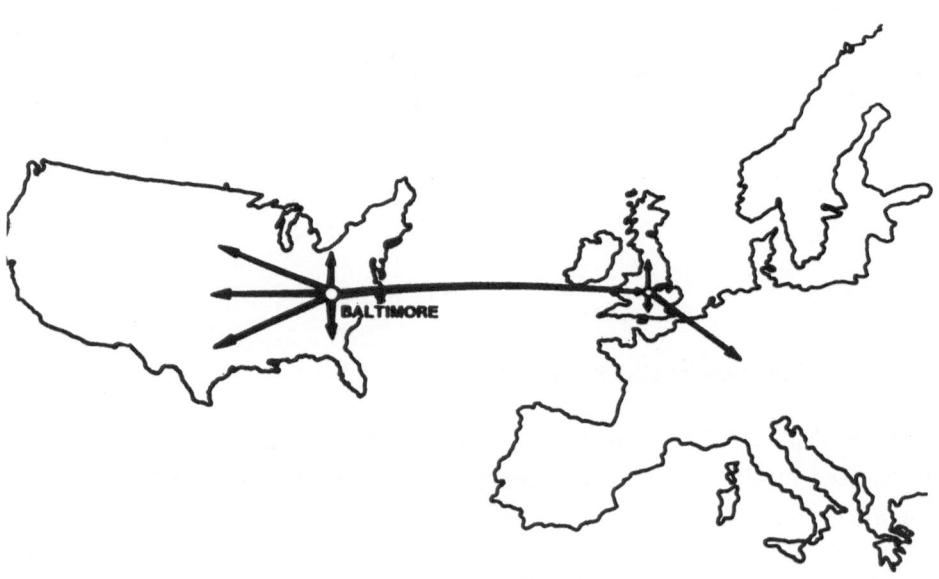

Figure 4.16: ENE88i and CNMA — June 1988.

All the exhibitors were interconnected through a Local Area Network. The LAN was linked through public packet facilities to manufacturers' parent plants throughout the USA and through international packet network facilities to a parallel European MAP/TOP conference in the UK (Birmingham), sponsored by the CNMA, SPAG, OSITOP and EMUG.

Visitors to ENE88i could send messages to any address in the UK via an X.400 gateway and a post room print facility, provided by ICL. Messages could be originated at almost every stand in the ENE88i exhibition and thus demonstrated the number of manufacturers that have implemented both the lower layer profiles and the upper layer X.400 profile set.

## Permanent Demonstrations

Other more permanent demonstrations of support are provided by OSI demonstrator groups around the world.

EurOSInet is a collaboration between the leading manufacturers in Europe to provide multi-vendor OSI demonstrations. The key USA manufacturers who operate in Europe are also members. The demonstrations include interconnection, using the connection oriented X.25 WAN profile, and interworking, using either the FTAM file transfer profile or the X.400 message handling profile.

OSInet is a similar collaboration between US manufacturers to provide multi-vendor demonstrations in the USA and similar multi-vendor OSI demonstration capabilities are being established in many other countries, such as OSIcom in Australia.

Functional standards have brought world-wide commitment and their adoption is creating new capabilities which will expand the European and global markets for IT systems.

# ICL COMMITMENT

## Policy Towards OSI

After reading the above sections you should be in no doubt about the ICL commitment to OSI and the company involvement both in the creation of the base standards and in the evolution of functional standards. Much of the early fundamental work on OSI can be traced back to ICL origins in the late 1960s and early 1970s.

The ICL architecture, known as the ICL Information Processing Architecture (IPA), already embodies OSI. ICL now has products in place which allow the smooth migration from the proprietary elements of IPA to the stable parts of OSI, without disrupting user service.

The ICL policy is to implement OSI in controlled phases, during which all the proprietary ICL solution elements will be replaced by totally OSI solutions.

The first phase is already being implemented and involves immediate alignment with the OSI interconnection profiles for CSMA/CD LAN and X.25 WAN and those application profiles which have already reached stability, such as X.400 and FTAM. This will be followed by the phased adoption of the other OSI applications as the standards stabilise.

Sufficient products are now in place to allow all ICL users to transfer to an all-OSI interconnection environment which uses CSMA/CD LANs and X.25 WAN protocols. The latter can be used either for packet network connections or to replace proprietary interconnection protocols on direct leased line connections.

X.400 message handling protocols have already been introduced into the ICL office product range and will be extended across the full Networked Product Line. FTAM is available on selected products and its availability is also being extended across the full networked product line (NPL).

Intercepts are being developed for other OSI standards, which are still within the standards agreement process, to minimise the introduction lead time when they are ratified.

ICL intends to play a lead role in the creation of the commonwealth of OSI products which will expand the European and global market for multi-vendor European solutions.

## Migration Policy

An ICL policy decision was made several years ago to introduce the OSI transport layer into IPA to act as a common bridge between the interworking and interconnection functions, regardless of whether proprietary or OSI protocols were being used.

The transport layer is now implemented across the whole of the ICL Networked Product Line and allows the well-established IPA applications and services to run over either proprietary interconnection or OSI interconnection services (refer back to figure 4.4). In migration terms, this means that any ICL user can install OSI interconnection now and continue to run the existing IPA applications and services until it is convenient to introduce the equivalent OSI applications. During the Migration phase, any OSI applications which are introduced can run alongside the traditional applications to avoid any disruption of service.

This leads to a simple phased OSI migration strategy for ICL users:

1.  introduce an OSI interconnection facility;

2.  continue to run existing applications and services to avoid disruption;

3.  introduce OSI applications alongside existing IPA applications;

4.  move to entirely OSI interconnection and applications.

It is ICL policy to develop an OSI migration plan for each ICL user and to extend this service to assist other non-ICL users to plan their migration route to the multi-vendor benefits of OSI.


# CONCLUSION

OSI standards have always been the desirable choice for multi-vendor systems, but the dramatic catalyst has been the functional standardisation process, begun by SPAG and MAP/TOP. The selection of a few clear options which meet practical needs has generated the required confidence that clear procurement specifications can be produced and that conformance can be guaranteed. This has stimulated the CEC, governments and users world-wide to adopt an OSI procurement policy which will have a major influence on the growth of European and global IT markets.

One thing is clear. A supply policy that is based on any strategy other than OSI compatibility would be suicidal!

# 5

# STANDARDISATION FOR OPEN SYSTEMS INTERCONNECTION: RECENT DEVELOPMENTS AND FUTURE DIRECTIONS

*N. Bush, Senior Consultant*

*B. Wood, Principal Consultant, SEMA Group PLC*

## INTRODUCTION

Starting in the International Organisation for Standardisation (ISO) in 1978 and now taken over by the newly established Joint Technical Committee 1 (JTC 1) of ISO and the IEC (International Electrotechnical Commission), standardisation for open systems interconnection (OSI) is now a maturing activity, both in terms of the development of the standards themselves and in terms of their use in IT systems and related equipment. Consequently, work on OSI standards can now be seen as progressing in four overlapped phases:

1.  completion of an initial set of communication standards;

2.  filling out/evolution of the initial set of communication standards;

3.  development of functional standards defining the use of the initial set of standards to meet particular needs;

4.  preparation for future developments.

# THE INITIAL SET OF OSI STANDARDS

The initial set of OSI standards covers the communications functions identified by the Basic Reference Model for OSI. The Reference Model prescribes a 7-layer subdivision of the functions required for communication between computer systems and a corresponding structure of OSI standards. In practice, in terms of the functions concerned, it is appropriate to regard the layers of the Reference Model as dividing into three groups.

The lower layers (1-4: Physical, Data Link, Network, and Transport) are concerned with the interconnection of end systems (computer systems) and data transfer between end systems. The standards of concern cover:

1.  access to subnetworks (transmission networks), comprising standards for local area networks (CSMA/CD, token bus, token ring, and slotted ring) and for wide area networks (eg X.25 based networks);

2.  support for the OSI Network Service over standard LANs and WANs, and (as a result) support for interconnection of end systems across concatenated subnetworks;

3.  provision of the Transport Service, giving specified qualities of service (error rates, throughput, cost etc.) over the data transfer paths provided by the Network Service.

Standards are agreed, or are close to agreement, for subnetwork access (LANs: CSMA/CD, token bus, token ring and slotted ring; WANs: X.25), for the Network Service and its provision, and for the Transport Service and its provision.

The standards for the next two layers (5 and 6, Session and Presentation) provide general functions to support the exchange of information between end systems using the data transfer facilities provided by the Transport Service:

1.  the Session standards provide means to structure the simple full-duplex Transport Service through procedures for dialogue control, for the exchange of synchronisation and resynchronisation signals, and for the resolution of protocol collisions;

2.  the Presentation standards define procedures for the exchange of information between end systems about the abstract syntax (logical structure) of the information to be exchanged, and for agreement on the transfer syntax (encoding)

to be used: they also define a standard notation (ASN.1) for the specification of abstract syntaxes and a corresponding encoding.

Both Session and Presentation standards have now been published by ISO.

Finally, the Application Layer standards provide for interworking between application processes in end systems (where an application process is a program or set of programs fulfilling some processing requirement within an end system eg. a branch accounting system for a bank or a control program in a factory). There are Application Layer standards agreed in four areas. These are:

1.   the File Transfer, Access and Management (FTAM) standard, allowing an application process in one end system to access and operate on files in a file store on another end system;

2.   the Messaging standards, defined by CCITT (in collaboration with ISO) in the X.400 (1984) Recommendations, specifying standards for the operation of, and for access to, store and forward messaging services;

3.   the Virtual Terminal (VT) standards, specifying communications procedures between terminal controllers and host computers for remote terminal access;

4.   initial versions of the Job Transfer and Manipulation (JTM) standards, specifying procedures to set up, and control asynchronous processing activities across a network of end systems.

Supplementing these service standards is the Office Document Architecture (ODA) standard. This is a multi-part standard which first defines a general architecture for specifying document structures and then, within that architecture, defines a general document interchange format and the ways in which different forms of content should be specified (character, raster graphics, geometric graphics). The early parts of this standard are agreed; the later ones are likely to reach agreement this year.

In addition there are standards for general facilities of importance for interworking:

1.   the Association Control Service Element (ACSE) standards, providing for the initialisation of communication between application processes, authentication of communicating partners, and agreement on the application protocols to be used for communication;

2.   the Commitment, Concurrency, and Recovery Service Element (CCR) standards, providing procedures for ensuring the integrity of a set of operations, possibly

involving application processes in a number of systems (for example, in the operation of the JTM procedures);

3. the Remote Operations Service Element (ROSE) standards, providing procedures to support interactive operations between application processes; and

4. the Reliable Transfer Service Element (RTSE) standards, providing procedures for recovery from end system failure during transmission.

ACSE has been agreed; CCR, ROSE and RTSE are in the final stages of agreement.


# CONSOLIDATION AND EVOLUTION

The set of standards outlined in the previous section provide essential communication tools, and it is becoming evident, through product announcements, that a majority of suppliers of IT equipment are now committed to implementation of a significant proportion of the set. A second phase of activity is now underway to consolidate, fill out and extend this initial set of standards.

In the first place, the initial set of standards needs extension:

1. for the lower four layers, to address new LAN technologies (eg. fibre distributed data interface - FDDI), to define the operation of interworking units linking subnetworks (in particular, exchanges of routing information), and to define ISDN operation;

2. for FTAM, to provide for more sophisticated file structures and more complex management needs - in particular to respond to the requirements from distributed office applications;

3. for VT, to provide terminal management procedures to support windowing and allow mixed mode operations;

4. for JTM, to provide a full service.

In the second place, there are functions concerned with supporting and controlling communications activities which must be addressed by standards if the basic communication standards are to be fully exploited. Activity in these areas is already underway:

1. for OSI Management, the Management Framework (Part 4 of the Basic Reference Model) has been agreed as a full International Standard, the first parts of the Management Information standards (covering common functions) are at the Draft Proposal stage, and further parts of the Management Information standards (covering faults, configuration, security, accounting, and the structure of management information) will reach the Draft Proposal stage early in 1989;

2. for Directory operation, the standard has been progressed in collaboration with CCITT, and common text for an ISO standard and a CCITT Recommendation was agreed at the end of 1988;

3. for Security, Part 2 of the Basic Reference Model, which defines a basic framework for providing security functions within OSI standards, is agreed, and work has begun on the definition of the detailed requirements for specific areas (authentication, access control, and non-repudiation).

Thirdly, work is now well underway on standards for Transaction Processing communications, the major area of communications standardisation not covered by existing work. Initial drafts for standards in this area have been developed, drawing heavily on supplier experience, and these are targeted to reach the Draft International Standard stage by the middle of 1989.

Finally, there is a clear need for agreed specifications of tests for conformance to the standards. In response to this need, a conformance test methodology standard is now well advanced and activity is starting on the standardisation of specific test suites.


## FUNCTIONAL STANDARDISATION

The standards that have been discussed in the previous sections are sometimes referred to as base (OSI) standards because they are defined with sets of optional features, choices of parameters etc. which allow them to be tailored to meet particular needs. Thus, base standards cannot be applied in isolation but must be applied in combination to support interworking between systems.

It is becoming increasingly clear that there is a need to complement the specification of base standards with functional standards: specifications of the use of base standards (with specific choices of options) in combination to support particular user, application, or system needs. A number of regional and industry initiatives are underway on functional standardisation:

1.  the activities of the Standards Promotion and Application Group (SPAG), a grouping of European IT suppliers which has developed and published a Guide to the Use of (OSI) Standards;

2.  the CEC sponsored activities of CEN/CENELEC/CEPT, building on the work of SPAG to develop European Functional Standards;

3.  the activity of the Implementors' Workshops, sponsored by the National Institute of Standards and Technology (NIST) in the USA, in the development of Implementation Agreements for Open Systems Interconnection Protocols;

4.  the establishment of a Conference for the Promotion of OSI (POSI) in Japan.

However, there has been understandable concern that these separate initiatives could result in divergent applications of the standards and the machinery is now being established to bring these together through JTC 1. A Special Group has been established within JTC 1 to develop International Standardised Profiles (ISPs) on the basis of proposals from the established groups. The Special Group was set up because the activity cuts across the areas of work of a number of existing subcommittees. It is defining the procedures to be followed in developing proposals for ISPs (to avoid duplication, ensure all interests are considered etc.) and in processing these proposals rapidly within ISO.

In some cases, there may be yet a further stage in specifying the application of the base standards which, although not a standardisation activity, is worth mentioning here for completeness. This is the specification of the use together of a set of profiles within particular system environments. Examples of this are the MAP (Manufacturing Automation Protocol), TOP (Technical and Office Protocol) and GOSIP (Government OSI Profile) specifications. The MAP and TOP specifications have been developed (originally by General Motors and Boeing Computer Services respectively, but now by MAP and TOP User Groups) to define the application of the NBS Implementation Agreements within the factory and office environment. The GOSIP specification is being developed (in collaboration with suppliers and other interested users) by the UK Central Computer and Telecommunications Agency (CCTA) to define the application of functional standards within the environment of government systems. Although currently a UK activity, the CCTA is maintaining close contact with corresponding government agencies in the US and Europe.

## FUTURE DIRECTIONS

OSI standards are directed at prescribing procedures for communication between end systems. In themselves they do not specify the effects of the communication within end systems (e.g. the FTAM protocol could be used to communicate with a remote printing device ). However, it is clear that the objective of communication using the OSI standards will be to support processing within end systems for specific applications. Such an objective is clearly implied by MAP, TOP, and GOSIP: these are intended to support the use of standards in the implementation of systems. This brings in much wider concerns than those addressed by OSI standardisation:

1.  specification of the processing associated with communication (e.g. changes to stored information);

2.  other areas of standardisation, in particular, database standards, standards for operating system functions, computer graphics standards (for the representation of complex information)....;

3.  system issues e.g. level of reliability/redundancy, transparency of system distribution...

Activity is already established in some of these areas (database and graphics standards) and is beginning in others (standards for operating system functions). However, there is a need for an overall framework to relate the areas of specific activity, to ensure their coherence, and to ensure that they can be used together to meet (distributed) processing requirements.

In recognition of this need, work is underway within JTC 1 to define a Reference Model of Open Distributed Processing, where the term open distributed processing (ODP) is introduced here, by analogy with open systems interconnection, to characterise distributed processing which exploits relevant standards (and therefore may be supported on equipment from different suppliers). Related activity for a specific application area is also taking place through work in the Office Systems area on a Distributed Office Applications Model.

JTC 1 has also established a technical study on Interfaces for Application Portability (IAP), looking at requirements for interface standards to be used by applications to access a set of system functions (including those addressed by current work on OSI, graphics, database etc.) with the objective of allowing portability of applications. Significant preparatory work has already been done in Japan, and the objectives of IAP standards seem strongly related to those of the portable common tool environment (PCTE) work in Europe.

Clearly, the work on ODP and IAP will set the agenda for the next major phase of Open Systems standardisation.


## ACKNOWLEDGEMENTS

This paper is a development and update of a paper published in the UK in the October 1987 issue of *Government Computing.*

# 6

# RELATIONAL DATABASE OPPORTUNITIES WITHIN THE SINGLE EUROPEAN MARKET: COMMITMENT TO STANDARDS AND OPEN SYSTEMS

*M. Eaton*

*Relational Technology Limited*

## INTRODUCTION

This paper will examine the business and marketing opportunities created by the Single European Market of 1992 and the challenges it raises for UK companies and their use of IT. The significance of Open Systems technology and adhering to technology standards that integrate different manufacturers' hardware and operating systems will be discussed. The importance of providing users with more information seamlessly across vast geographical areas, using highly flexible distributed relational database technology and fourth generation languages, will also be detailed.

All businesses wanting to take full advantage of the European market opportunities cannot afford to ignore its technology requirements and, if they have not already done so, must start to address these requirements in the light of their own business strategies and product developments.

## Removing the Barriers and Facing the Competition

By 31st December 1992, the twelve member countries of the European Community will have become the Single European Market. The progressive removal of trade barriers will create an open market for goods and services, access to some 325 million consumers, and an international source of capital and human skills.

Industry analysts see the post-1992 European market as a more competitive environment in which the successful participants will be those who, throughout Europe, have the most up to date and effective information to hand.

With the onset of 1992, user requirements are swiftly being re-evaluated, and hardware and software IT suppliers will have to address these changes by offering more comprehensive networking strategies and more accessible software systems which will need to run uniformly across and increasingly broad range of hardware. As the full implications of the Single European Market become clear, users will increasingly need to gain access to greater amounts of data, to instigate more multi-location development projects and develop account co-ordination facilities.

Although the 31st December 1992 deadline has been set, there will continue to be barriers to negotiate. As well as legal and language differences, only a quarter of the directives needed to remove all non-tariff barriers have been approved to date. Each directive has to be passed by individual acts of parliament in each of the countries, so it is unlikely that all will have been ratified by the 1992 deadline.

## The Opportunities

As barriers to trade are progressively removed in the run-up to 1992 and beyond, UK companies will have new opportunities to bring their product offerings to a wider market place. According to a recently published CBI report, nearly a third of Britain's major companies have yet to do anything specific for 1992, whilst others have clear 1992 business strategies and have already started to organise their operations to address the Single European Market. They are forming international partnerships and distributorships, and acquiring or setting up trans-European companies to better place themselves to make the most of new market opportunities and to develop new strategies to meet the new competition in their home market.

At the product level, companies must set themselves to understand and meet the requirements of the new markets they intend to enter.

The European market will demand instant access to more, geographically dispersed, information in order for companies to take full advantage of new and changing market opportunities. To meet this requirement, companies must be able to deliver highly flexible applications systems and supporting technologies that operate across numerous hardware platforms and operating systems and over broader geographical areas. The systems will have to offer users the maximum in end-user flexibility to allow them to work with different countries' tax laws, trading laws and even languages. The systems themselves must be easy to modify and upgrade as market shifts are mirrored in changing user requirements.

This will lead to users demanding non-proprietary systems which integrate their existing data resources, enabling organisations with Europe-wide interests to work on distributed development projects, and interchange data electronically.

The technology that meets these requirements will provide the infra-structure to enable the European Single Market to flourish. Suppliers however must adhere to common European operating standards and open systems.

## OPEN SYSTEMS AND STANDARDS

Much of the impetus for the development of the necessary open systems and standards has come from within Europe. Organisations such as X/Open and the Open Software Foundation have been established to enable users to interconnect their incompatible hardware systems, freeing them from long-term commitments to single hardware suppliers, protecting their hardware and software investments and providing a basis for integrated business development and computer strategies.

## OSI

Serious work was begun in 1977 by the International Standards Organisation, ISO, technical committee. Since then, much has been done to define the contents of the seven levels of the Open Systems Interconnection, OSI, model, which is a framework for the classification and development of protocols. The basic premise of the OSI model is to define which communications functions are to be handled by the individual layers.

The existence of the model is, in itself, not sufficient to ensure its successful implementation. Much of the pressure for the adoption of OSI has come from large governmental and commercial organisations who require greater interconnectivity. This has led to government directives that networking purchases should conform to OSI standards, and in 1987 the EEC ruled that any IT purchase of over £70,000 should incorporate OSI specifications.

This pressure is particularly pronounced in Europe, with small national markets comprising diverse languages and cultures. In 1983, for example, the Standards Promotion and Applications Group, SPAG, was founded by twelve European computer manufacturers with a joint objective to formulate, promote and implement OSI standards. At the end of 1987, the Europeans were joined by DEC, Hewlett-Packard, and IBM, taking the Open Systems initiative to the international market.

By late 1988, standards for layers one to four of the OSI model were available, with the lowest three being most clearly defined and in common use. Level four, transport, and level five, session, were near to completion, with practical testing and clarification underway. As yet ISO standards above level five are non-existent. Testing of the protocols for all seven layers of the OSI model, however, is expected to be completed well before 1992 according to industry experts.

## X/Open

Although OSI is unquestionably a good standard, its value is limited to promoting physical connectivity and communication between different hardware environments. Users in Europe also need non-proprietary Open Systems that ensure the portability of their applications over hardware platforms supplied by different vendors. The cost of retraining in the event of vendor changes, as well as software maintenance, would all be minimised because of the consistency of the user interface regardless of underlying hardware.

X/Open, founded in 1984 is dedicated to the creation of an internationally supported, vendor independent, common applications environment based on industry standards. To this end it has developed a branding program to provide a common set of programming interfaces to UNIX based operating system services. The standards it has and will adopt are all culled from existing, widely supported official and de facto standards, including the portable operating system POSIX, and C and other ANSI standard programming languages.

By adhering to such standards, technology vendors will be committing themselves to a strategy that will give them access to significantly larger market bases, and that will give users the kind of systems that the Single European Market demands.

## DISTRIBUTED DATABASES — THE WAY FORWARD

Nowhere is this standardisation more important than in the field of corporate information databases.

To make the best use of their resources companies must be able to concurrently access, manipulate and update their corporate information. It will not be enough for an organisation to have separate databases in Paris, in London and in Rome. These will need to be fully integrated and fully accessible from anyshere in Europe. Relational database technology is essential, but it will also have to be fully distributed, and be able to operate across the broadest range of hardware architectures.

To fully protect hardware and software investments, the systems must also be easy to maintain and update as changes in the market are reflected in changes in user requirements. The relational database should therefore also contain a fourth generation language, that allows programmers to quickly and easily write additional routines into applications and provide the flexibility to tailor the end-user environment for each country concerned.

### Distributed Processing or Distributed Databases?

It is important to distinguish between distributed processing and distributed databases. The former allows applications in a network, to access a single database residing on a mainframe or minicomputer. By contrast, a distributed database system gives access to many physical databases on any number of computers simultaneously, bringing together the different islands of information that inevitably exist within any multi-site or multi-national computer system. This allows users anywhere in the organisation to access data regardless of on what computer hardware, operating system, database systems or file systems the data resides as if it was one local database.

Complete distributed relational database management systems require four elements: portability, connectivity, distributed data management and data gateway technology.

Portability allows major organisations, which normally have multiple computer environments, to use the same database management system and tools across different environments. For international corporations attempting to integrate their deverse operations into a comprehensive Pan-European Strategy, this facility allows users to run applications unchanged across a number of platforms, reducing program development and training costs.

Connectivity allows users to run applications on one system to access data on another, regardless of differences in hardware or operating systems. Distributed data management offers users the capability to access data stored at several locations simultaneously, and use the data as a unified information resource. Such distributed systems enable systems managers to manage the data at these diverse sources without individual users having to know where the data actually resides.

Data gateway technology will allow relational database applications to access data from existing applications that use early generation file management systems, maintaining their functionality. This painless migration is valuable to Pan-European users as it ensures the continuity of familiar and well-maintained old systems, without having to modify the programming and data administration routines already established by separate computer operations.

## Transparency is the Key

An effectice distributed database system will enable relatively unsophisticated users to create complex queries, request data from a number of different locations, and will free users and applications programmers from needing to know where data is physically located. The next stage will be the assimilation of global data dictionaries and distributed CASE (Computer-Aided Software Engineering) tools into the programmer's armoury of software development tools, allowing the integrated planning of new applications and systems, and enhance distributed development projects.

Ahead of its competitors, Relational Technology has developed a distributed database solution with applications which can transparently access data from remote systems. Using Ingres/Star, Relational Technology's distributed database system, a sales manager in Rome could compile a report based on data gathered from branch offices in each of the other eleven European community member nations, based on only one initial data request.

## CATERING FOR MULTIPLE HARDWARE USERS

Ingres and Ingres/Star are based on an open architecture which ensures that existing valuable data can be integrated with the latest systems. Ingres offers gateways to DEC's Rdb, RMS and dBASE III, and is actively working on gateways to DB/2, SQL/DS, IMS, IDMS and VSAM.

Ingres supports a wide variety of hardware platforms, including IBM, ICL and DEC, UNIX-based minicomputers and workstations and all DOS-based PCs.

## MAXIMISING EUROPEAN SYSTEMS FLEXIBILITY

A fully integrated computer network spanning Europe will be subject to constant changes in user requirements. It is critical therefore that the whole system be easy to update and maintain. This flexibility can be achieved with a full-function fourth generation language capability built into the integrated relational database package.

Ingres is the only distributed relational system to combine a fourth generation language with a powerful interactive development environment. Application development is much faster than with conventional third generation language development and the mundane aspect of applications maintenance, which currently accounts for up to 80 per cent of skilled programmers' resources, is dramatically reduced.

## SUMMARY

The Single European Market will open up major new market opportunities for UK companies. That will open up major new market opportunities for UK technology companies. Central to these requirements is the need for instant access up-to-the-minute information held on any number of geographically and physically different manufacturers' systems.

Almost all users, particularly those in government, finance and manufacturing, are now convinced of the benefits of integrating all structures, and more importantly, integrating them so that they can work as one.

This will lead to continued demand for OSI, non-proprietary operating systems, portable 4GLs and distributed databases, a demand that Relational Technology is ideally placed to meet.

# 7

# PROPRIETARY AND PUBLIC STANDARDS

*P.W.L.Morgan*

*Director of Corporate Services, IBM United Kingdom Ltd.*

When the organisers of this conference first approached me they suggested that my subject should be from proprietary to public standards. I chose not to speak on that exact theme because I could not have supported the general direction implied. But strange as it may seem I cannot address even the rather bland title of *Proprietary and Public Standards* without some important qualification.

In the strict legal sense, there is no such thing as a **proprietary standard** because it is not possible to own standards, architectures or information per se. These are always in the public domain. It is possible to have certain rights to the exclusive use of ideas registered as patents, and rights over the reproduction and use of copyright documents. It is possible to own intellectual property - but it is not possible to own the related information. The term proprietary standard is however very widely used in the trade press - but I would argue that there are no proprietary standards as such.

The term **public standard** also needs clarification because it is ambiguous. There are standards which are intended for use by those providing a public service. I am thinking specifically of those developed in CCITT and CEPT. There are others, such as product and environmental safety standards, which public authorities enforce by statute. But I suspect that when the conference organisers invited me to prepare this paper, their concept of public standards was not limited to such specifics.

After so many disclaimers, I should define my approach:- what I intend to address is the question of when and why a major supplier chooses to base his products on technical specifications defined by his own development operation, and when and why he chooses to augment those specifications by the use of standards developed by users and suppliers working in the national and international standards making bodies. I shall refer to the latter as **industry standards,** and the former as **supplier specifications.**

This paper will deal with a number of standards related topics, such as the role of government, the growth of user and supplier interest groups, the phenomenon of so-called de facto standards, and the topical question of organisation of the standards process. But there are three important themes on which the paper focus.

My first thesis is that IBM, and all other major reputable suppliers, voluntarily and positively engage in the standards making process for sound commercial reasons, and do so to achieve benefits that are not available by any other means.

My second thesis is that it is important for the user, and for government, to understand the advantages and the limitations of industry standards, because otherwise unrealistic expectations may occur, which may hold back the phenomenal rate of technological change from which the user has reaped enormous benefit.

My third point is that if the standardisation process is to produce the benefits of which it is undoubtedly capable, then some drastic changes are necessary in the organisation of standards work both in this country and at the international level.

Returning then to my first point - the adoption by IT suppliers of industry standards to replace or supplement supplier specifications is not a new phenomenon. It is something which has happened throughout the history of the Information Technology industry (e.g. Comtran v COBOL, EBCDIC v ASCII), because both industry standards and supplier specifications have an indispensable part to play if information technology is to reach its full potential.

OSI is a useful case in point as is IBM's part in it. Contrary to popular belief, it is an area in which IBM has played a leading role in both the development of the standards and the implementation of those standards in products. Commentators have often implied that IBM would not embrace OSI because it might weaken the position of IBM's own network architecture, SNA. Yet IBM has devoted more resource than any other single company to the hard detailed work that is carried on in the OSI working groups and committees of the national and international standards bodies. In addition there has been extensive IBM activity designed to facilitate implementation or promote the use of OSI through membership of organisations like OSINET in the US, EUROSINET in the UK, the Hanover Fair demonstrations of X.400 messaging, the NCC coordinated UK Joint Project for the development of OSI Conformance test tools, and membership of the committees which developed the CCTA GOSIP specification. IBM offered the world's first Open Systems Verification Service from our laboratory in La Gaude. All this is in addition to active IBM participation in organisations such as COS, MAP, TOP, OSITOP and more recently SPAG Services.

At the same time, through the 1980s, IBM announced the availability of a steady stream of OSI products. As early as 1984 we were the first major supplier to provide a capability to implement OSI Systems up to the top of layer 5. (Open Transport and Session Services (OTSS) with Open Systems Network Support (OSNS)). Since then we have extended this capability to layer 7 with Messaging and File Transfer facilities.

In September 1988 IBM made further announcements, of which two aspects must be highlighted.

1.  The network management products that were announced will be the first from any known source to me to implement the new OSI Directory & OSI Management draft international standards (ISO DP 9596-2, ISO DIS 9594 and CCITT X.519)

2.  IBM also announced that OSI standards would form part of the specification for its Systems Application Architecture (SAA), along with the specifications for IBM's other communications architecture, SNA.

The significance of the last point is two-fold.

1.  First, that in IBM's view the OSI standards are sufficiently stable and complete, and the market requirement sufficiently mature, to justify the inclusion of OSI specifications in their major strategic architecture. The commitment to supply OSI products has always been subject to a proviso that IBM would do so only to the extent that was judged the specification in the standard to be technically viable and stable, and the market was judged to be strong enough to justify the investment.

2.  Secondly, and perhaps more relevant to the theme of this paper, IBM once again underlined its view that OSI and SNA have different objectives. On the one hand SNA is designed to provide the optimum communications performance in an environment where the system is homogeneous, i.e. the fruits of the development work of one supplier. On the other hand, according to the ISO document which describes the overall OSI model (IS 7498), OSI is designed to facilitate communication between Open Systems, i.e. systems developed according to many

different suppliers specifications, as long as they offer an Open Systems communications facility.

IBM have always maintained that many users will benefit from the ability to call up either set of facilities according to the circumstances. The notion that products must be based on either a supplier's specification or on industry standards is a myth. If you can use them both, and they each offer unique benefits of value to you, why not have both?

This OSI illustration brings out rather well the distinction between supplier specifications and industry standards. First, certain desirable attributes of IT products can only be guaranteed through the use of supplier specifications, for example:

1. optimum performance

2. maximum function

3. state of the art implementation

4. maximum accountability.

These are the attributes which customers expect when they use SNA for communication purposes. They should not expect them from products based solely on industry standards. This is because of the heterogeneous nature of the range of different manufacturers machines that have to be accommodated, because of the inevitable delays inherent in the consensus based international industry standards-making process, and because of the state of the art of standards writing and conformance testing.

On the other hand there are desirable attributes which can only be achieved through the use of agreed industry standards. Examples include:

1. universal information exchange (ASCI, OSI, ODA, EDI)

2. common end-user interfaces (keyboards, symbols)

3. wide physical connectability

4. wide portability of supplies

5. wide portability of software

6. protection of individuals and environment.

In these areas the benefits accrue only when there is a consensus which leads all or a substantial majority of suppliers to implement the standard. It follows however that use of the standard cannot provide any competitive advantage. You may therefore question the business rationale suppliers use for devoting resources to the development of such standards. IBM's rationale, and I presume that of all suppliers who contribute to industry standards making is that if we can establish the consensus which provides the desirable attributes listed above, and which conversely cannot be provided without that consensus, they will increase the take-up of our products and the size of the total Information Technology market. It is then up to each supplier to compete in product or marketing terms to obtain his share of that expanded market.

However, the fact that a standard has been agreed internationally does not guarantee that it will be adopted by suppliers. Ultimately the success of any supplier depends on his ability to satisfy customer requirements, and so a supplier will adopt industry standards only to the extent, and at the time, that the market determines. A supplier will maintain and extend the unique attributes of his own systems as long as he see a marketing advantage, in order to differentiate himself from other supplier. That is as it should be in a free society where business is based on economic competition and market forces.

That then is the first theme - that for sound business reasons suppliers can be both enthusiastic supporters of the industry standards making process, whilst continuing to develop differentiated capabilities through their own R&D.

Turning to the second theme - the threat to innovation - I have already argued against the evolutionary theory which suggests that all supplier specifications will be gradually replaced by publicly developed industry standards, but I would like to comment in parenthesis that if such an evolution were achieved it would not be in the best interests of either the European supply industry or the user. With a totally standardised product, and competition reduced to cost, quality and delivery, the European supply industry might find itself in difficulty, unable to compete with far-eastern production, and so reduced to badge engineering, as has been the case in other sectors of the electronics industry.

In such a situation, and faced with the strategic need to maintain a European IT manufacturing capacity, protectionism could reassert itself. And with a protected and standardised product the supply industry could quickly come to resemble that section of the electronics industry which in the past supplied PTTs network switches. For all its technical excellence, that sector did not have a good reputation for the speed at which it has brought the benefits of new technology to the user. I acknowledge that this cautionary tale is hypothetical, but surely it is essential for the health of the European IT industry, and for the ultimate benefit of the user, that we do not allow a passion for standardisation to remove the incentive to innovate and invent.

Even in the absence of a totally standardised product there is a danger that the bureaucrat, in pursuit of industrial policy or trade harmonisation objectives, will press for a level of standardisation which fails to recognise the legitimate limitations to that process. Confining standardisation to the achievement of those user benefits which cannot be achieved by any other means is an important principle in a free market economy. It is the only possible justification for an activity which requires competing companies to meet and exchange knowledge of market requirements and technical know-how - activity which in any other circumstances is essentially anti-competitive.

Given that industry standards are, or should be, about providing benefits to users, who should be involved in developing those standards? The answer is:

1.  those interests which can reliably assess the user benefit and

2.  those interests which can assess the implementation cost.

What about government? Does it have a role? It is fashionable these days in governmental circles to talk of promoting an open market by levelling the playing field, and using standards as part of this levelling process. Such a policy must involve measures which have the effect of second guessing the process of market selection and I have difficulty in distinguishing such a policy from the now discredited policy of picking winners. Government involvement which is directed towards manipulating the market, rather than involvement as a significant user, will at best slow down the process of achieving consensus. At worst it will result in standards which do not have as their principal objective the optimum benefit for the user.

Turning now to the third point - the organisation of the standards making process. We start by examining further the paradox that while some industry standards are adopted by the supply industry others are ignored. It has been already shown that the principal determinant of whether a standard is implemented is the market need. When effort is put into the development of standards which the market place then does not adopt, there is a waste of resource which we would all like to avoid. On occasions this can be due to the fact that standardisation projects have not always followed the principle of maximum user benefit, but there are other reasons, particularly timing. In the industry standards-making process timing is critical. If the standard is too early, before the technology is stable, it will be overtaken by the changing technology and products based on the standard will find no place in the market. If it is too late, then there is a risk that the market will adopt with enthusiasm a particular manufacturers' specification which becomes, in the jargon of the trade press, a de facto standard. The IBM PC was one such example. It was so successful that it became established as a de facto standard even though it was clearly outside the orthodox IBM corporate architecture, let alone any consideration of industry standards. (Since then we have further developed our PC products with Micro Channel Architecture and OS/2, and brought them into our SAA scheme.)

Timing is so critical in standards making that some people have questioned the efficacy of the present international standards-making process. It is of particular concern to the users who wish to avail themselves of the benefits of standardisation. It is of great concern to those elements of the supply industry who, having little or no development effort of their own, are obliged to rely exclusively on offering products which meet industry standards. It is also of concern to any supplier who puts considerable amounts of resource into the process because extended time scales tie up that highly skilled resource.

But achieving world wide consensus is not an easy task. It involves the coordination of views of sometimes hundreds of experts and special interest representatives working in standards committees, sub-committees, panels and working groups in national, regional and international standards bodies, trade associations and user groups. The necessary consultation processes between each of those levels and areas of interest require time scales which inevitably result in standards which lag behind the technology. The process of maintenance of the standards adds further delays.

The concern of those who want to speed up the process has led to the recent phenomenon of a mushrooming of groups to promote the development, adoption, and implementation of various categories of industry standards. They include SPAG, COS, MAP, TOP, EMUG, ISOTOP, OSINET, EUROSINET, Uniforum, X/Open, OSF, UNIX International and EISA. Some have originated in the user community e.g. MAP, TOP, and their European counterparts EMUG and ISOTOP, and in the UNIX world Uniforum. Others originate in a section of the supply industry which feels that it has a particular interest in promoting one set of standard specifications - groups such as SPAG, COS, X/Open, OSF and UNIX International. But a very interesting characteristic of these groups is that although they frequently start life promoting the particular standards interest of one group, they ultimately open their doors to membership right across the industry, embracing supplier and user interests. The reason for this is obvious and supports the argument above: - industry standards have their value not in providing state of the art technology, but in providing certain desirable attributes which are present only if their is wide consensus and implementation. Ideally the consensus is achieved through a formal process. If however a formal consensus is unachievable, but the user benefit is sufficiently compelling, the market will dictate the standard. It is for these reasons that we can expect that the differences which now exist between OSF and UNIX International will be resolved, even though the most recent discussions have stalled. However, too much delay will mean that the market place makes the choice for them.

We should not imply, like Candide, that all is for the best in the best of all possible worlds. We must not be complacent about the formal standards-making process. It is clearly preferable that it should be capable of anticipating the market, bringing forward the benefits of standardisation. After all, it was precisely because of the chaos caused by the proliferation of organisations and trade associations purporting to develop and endorse standards, that the national bodies such as BSI, AFNOR, DIN (Deutsche Institut für Normalschung) and ANSI, and the international bodies such as ISO and IEC, were created in the first place. There is a current debate both at the national and the European level about the most appropriate structure for the standards-making process. This is a fruitful area for government involvement, because government can legislate the required mechanisms into existence at the national level, and through diplomacy make things happen at the international level.

As a member of the UK government's FOCUS committee I am pleased to have been party to the decision to recommend to the DTI the need for the most radical restructuring of the standards making process that the venerable BSI will ever have experienced - the creation of an IT Standards Institute that we hope will make the standards-making process more responsive to the needs of the market place. We will return to the question of the European structure later.

And so to examine the question - where next? The last thirty years have seen the continuing phenomena of rapidly falling hardware costs coupled with escalating software development costs. User pressures to counter the latter trend have had impacts in three areas of standardisation:

1.  programming languages for enhanced programmer productivity in terms of the number of lines of object code generated

2.  quality management systems to enhance productivity in terms of reduced need for rewrites

3.  portability to extend the active life of code through hardware upgrades and across suppliers' systems.

Back in the 1950s and 1960s we had high hopes that high level programming language standardisation would also lead to portability, but we all now recognise that in the present state of the art the idiosyncrasy of the underlying operating system is an important factor that we have to accommodate.

One approach - characterised by the POSIX effort which started in Uniforum and continues in IEEE 1003 and ISO/IEC JTC 1 is to standardise on one type of operating system. IBM has responded to this market requirement with a commitment to produce a set of products (the AIX family) already offering most of the features required by the X/Open Common Applications Environment specification. As conformance requirements are specified, and test suites developed, it is our intention to submit the AIX products for testing for conformance to the POSIX standards. IBM's ability to prove conformance will be helped in no small measure by the fact that it has had representatives in the working groups of IEEE since the inception of the POSIX work, and before that in the standards committees of Uniforum where the POSIX work started.

This approach will undoubtedly help some users to lower their software costs. It will be particularly significant because UNIX-like operating systems are already very popular and widely used in organisations with multiple vendor installations, where additional software portability can bring immediate substantial user benefit. However, I believe that in order to achieve the greatest range of capability at viable cost/performance ratios, it will be necessary for many years to use a range of hardware designs. And consequently, to achieve optimum performance, suppliers will continue to offer their own operating systems tailored to those hardware implementations. Those users who opt for the supplier operating system will nevertheless wish to minimise their software procurement and development costs through portability.

To meet this requirement IBM has embarked upon a two prong strategy. IBM's AIX products, and their co-operation with others in X/Open and OSF (the Open

Software Foundation) is intended to provide portability across UNIX-like operating systems. At the same time, to meet another element of the same user requirement they have also introduced SAA (Systems Application Architecture), to provide portability across three of IBM's most widely used operating environments. It is planned that there will be communications and language linkages between AIX and SAA.

JTC 1 Strategic Planning Group has also recognised a user requirement for the advantages of portability without the requirement to be tied to one operating system specification, and last April authorised the commencement of a study which it is hoped will lead in due course to the development of the necessary standards to permit portability, whilst allowing freedom to the user to choose the most suitable operating system for the hardware implementation and the application requirement. This project has the potential to become more significant in the development of the effective use of Information Technology than either the POSIX or the OSI projects which have occupied the industry for the last decade. It is IBM's intention to contribute to this work on the basis of its experience in implementing SAA.

Finally, a few words about IT standards and 1992. The significance of 1992 for our future well-being in Europe cannot and should not be underestimated. In many spheres of economic activity, the role that standards have to play is vital to the removal of technical barriers to trade within Europe. In the wider IT industry - i.e. using the term to embrace Telecommunications as well as the old EDP industry - an important initiative has been taken in the last two years through the creation of ETSI (European Telecommunication Standards Institute) for which the Commission is to be congratulated. The relative openness of that institution, compared with the previous arrangements, and the implementation of proposals under which task groups of professionals seconded to ETSI will work on projects for months at a time, should go a long way to ensure that the barriers erected, either deliberately or inadvertently, between the various national networks will quickly disappear and the providers of telecommunications services enabled to play a constructive role in the development of the new European economy.

By contrast the traditional EDP industry faces few technical barriers to the completion of the single European market. There are some small differences in the regulations in various countries in areas such as electrical safety, electro-magnetic interference and acoustic noise which the Commission is taking steps to harmonise, but these have not in the past been serious barriers since most of the industry sets itself higher standards than the regulations require.

Standards in the area of OSI and EDI will have a beneficial effect on the speed with which we can enjoy the benefits of the new open European economy, but these are efforts which have been in train for many years at an international level, and are not 1992 inspired, though they may be 1992 assisted. The reason that there are so few impediments for the traditional EDP industry in trading across European boundaries is the universal recognition for many years that our markets are international, our sources of supply are international, and our industry standards therefore must be international.

One small problem that has not been mentioned but which does add cost for the EDP industry trading in Europe is of course language - adding costs to keyboards and software products. That is a problem that will not go away in 1992 despite all the efforts of, the Commission, or the standards bodies. Frankly, it is a small price to pay for protecting the diversity of our European cultural heritage.

In conclusion, let us restate the argument - supplier specifications and industry standards both have their place. The advantages of innovation through suppliers specification on the one hand, and market growth through industry standards on the other, both make good business sense to user and supplier. There is no natural progression by which one ousts the other. They are complementary activities - each has its place.

Suppliers are enthusiastic supporters of standards making. Users are beneficiaries. Governments are best involved as users, and as detached facilitators of the process.

The way seems fairly clear for European standards making in the 1992 context. We are opposed to any fortress Europe distortion of standards - nothing but international standards will do.

The big future opportunity in IT standards making is application portability. UNIX alone cannot be the complete answer. Increasingly the standards process will become preoccupied by the search for that answer. IBM will be an enthusiastic partner in that search.

# Part Three

# User Case Studies of
# Open Systems and Interworking

Part Three

# User Case Studies

## Expert Systems and Interactions

# 8

# WHY OPEN SYSTEMS - A MANAGEMENT PERSPECTIVE

*C. V. Calder*

*General Manager Information Technology*
*The Automobile Association*

## BACKGROUND

The AA became involved in computing in 1964 with the purchase of its first mainframe computer. Like many other organisations, the Association continued to grow the mainframe systems by using proprietary products. By 1987 however, it had become obvious that things had to change, and it was perceived that a new strategy was needed, a framework within which to base decisions on IT investments, and by which to address the increasing business requirements of the AA.

The first and undoubtedly the most important were the changes in the business environment of the AA's major revenue earning activity, AA insurance services (AAIS) and their changing attitude to it.

Until the mid 1980s computing in the AA had been used to support the major corporate paper handling functions. It was mostly administrative. Whereas 70% of the AA's workforce had direct contact with customers, they had little or no IT support.

The 1987 Business Plan for Insurance, which incidentally was one of their first business plans that had a horizon of over 30 months, set out a requirement to change the external business environment away from a price sensitive buying scenario to a situation where the key product differentiator is customer service. AAIS were planning a huge increase in number of high street outlets and customer telephone answering facilities.

The second major factor was change in the IT environment. The proprietary approach of the 1970s and early 1980s had been eroded away by standardisation.

Products existed in the market place designed to support ISO standards for Open Systems Interconnection,

For personal computing and workstation, MSDOS had emerged as the de facto standard, and for multi-user, multi-tasking departmental systems, UNIX was and is the rising star.

The third force at play was the opportunity afforded by the AA's investment in a corporate voice and data network.

During 1986/87 a private voice network based upon digital PABXs had been implemented which had saved about £600,000 per year while at the same time providing a vast amount of bandwidth for data that could be justified on voice cost savings alone.

The fourth force at the time was an assessment of the role and deliverables of Management Services.

Up until 1987 Management Services were perceived to have a single supplier policy. Although this was true in terms of corporate computing, (totally ICL), it was not true in other areas. From the mid 1980s word processors were deliberately purchased from a number of different sources. Also the network itself, in terms of voice switches, modems, packet switched exchanges, LAN systems and so on was supplied by over a dozen different vendors. In any event the perception from the top of the organisation was that of a single supplier policy.

This corporate decision had a number of consequences. On the plus side a single set of skills were needed, and decisions were constrained to being able to support systems on the current range of hardware. More over, there was one supplier to kick, a single supplier who may by no means be the biggest in the world, but to whom the AA was a major account.

On the downside, the AA was constrained to a very small portfolio of packaged software and products from a supplier whose business objectives were perceived no longer to cover our expanding range of requirements.

At the same time the costs of delivery of systems were seen by the users to be increasing. 90% of Management Services spend had been underwritten by the businesses since 1985. Equally the cost of replacing old hardware with new hardware was escalating year on year as the terminal population grew, causing concern for the future. Although Management Services were using their considerable purchasing power for leverage in negotiating substantial discounts and driving suppliers into performance related contracts, this on its own was felt to be insufficient for the future.

Alongside all this, Management Services Group themselves were responding to the changing IT environment also with a major change in attitude. Our view of the mainframe changed, from being the solution for everything to being one of the horses for only one of the courses. A few members of the group saw the potential of the PC as an intelligent networked workstation, and not just a free standing personal computer, the way it had always been looked upon in the past.

## BUILDING A STRATEGY

Having acknowledged the need to change, and that the time was right, the question was how to do it.

The solution was an overall Information Systems (IS) and Information Technology (IT) strategy for the AA based upon Open Systems.

The first stage was to put together the business plans of the AA businesses and create a business plan for Management Services. This was when Management Services really started to believe that they were an integral business within the AA rather than some external bureau.

The distillation of the business plans produced four key business requirements that must be met by IT investments.

1. **Flexibility and expandability.** With the expansion of the AA's business especially in the high street, there would be a large and growing terminal population. These terminals would require access to a range of services and databases in different locations.

2. **Customer Oriented approach.** With the move to improved customer service increasing emphasis would be placed on good communications and controlled ease of access to data.

3. **Decrease the time to market.** In terms of systems development it was essential to increase the productivity of the development process, to produce better systems faster so as to be able to get the maximum return on any investment.

4.  **Reduced costs.** There are two underlying factors to reducing the costs. The first was to address the area of capital spend, not necessarily to reduce it but to strike the most cost-effective deals. The second was to reduce the problem of growing replacement costs by extending the operational life of products to 60 months.

All of these are in some way related, especially reducing costs and decreasing the time to market. If the time from the requirement to the delivered solution is reduced, there is a much better chance of extending the life of the system. Also, Management Services are seen to be more reactive, and competitive advantage is sustained longer.

The next stage was to underpin these business requirements with a set of technical objectives for the strategy.

1.  **Supplier independence.** Independence from the source of supply for IT will allow the AA to buy the most competitive offerings available on the market. Architectural platforms need to be specified which will allow hardware, software, network technology, consultancy and training to be independently and severally sourced. In this way the only player in the game with leverage is the AA itself.

2.  **Application Portability.** In order to reduce development costs and attain an average of 60 months operational use, architectural platforms are required to allow applications to be portable at the business level, the source code level and at the binary level wherever possible. In this way application life times can be de-coupled from hardware and operating system life cycles.

3.  **Single Network Connection.** To reduce the cost of service and give the ability to access different databases in different locations, a network architecture needs to be developed, whereby access to all AA and external services is via a single network connection. In this way the network can be used to deliver added value rather than just incremental costs.

4.  **A Standard User Interface.** To contain both user training and development costs, the architecture must address the use of a standard user menu for access to services. In this way services can be migrated and new services added with minimum disruption to the business or the need for significant retraining of staff.

5.  **Local Information processing.** By providing intelligent devices at the point of business, data communications costs will be minimised and dependence upon the network reduced.

6. **Growth.** The strategy must provide a cost-effective platform for growing both the user and service population and must in no way preclude any of the AA's future business plans.

7. **Security.** The approach must provide a framework within which security policy decisions can be made covering data integrity, access control, distribution of data and code, public network access etc.

8. **Data.** The strategy must address the definition, location, ownership and use of data throughout the AA.

9. **Operability.** A cost effective, flexible and easily managed environment must be created by the strategy. This will allow the controlled management of change, ease of implementation, speed of response and improved systems reliability.

10. **Networking.** The approach must address the integration management and control of voice and data. It must supply a platform for providing value added services and gateways to pan European services.

The next stage was to develop an overall architecture that addressed the technical requirements and thereby fulfilled the business plans. The role of the overall architecture is to provide a framework within which all developments and investments will be reviewed. This architecture is divided into a number of separate but related architectural layers.

1. The **Voice/Data Network Architecture** addresses the strategic objectives of Supplier Independence, Single Network Connection, Growth, Operability and Networking. It deals with the standards and technologies for building, interconnecting and managing networks. It comprises a set of rules by which network technologies will be integrated to provide the transparent passage of information within and between sites. This architecture describes the framework within which the AA's own network will be built and evolve.

   The basis of the Voice/Data Network Architecture is the adoption, implementation and integration of technologies built to international standards.

2. The **Service Architecture** addresses the strategic requirements of Operability, Supplier Independence and some of the requirements for Local Information Processing. It defines a set of standard interfaces through which users, management systems and business applications can access both local and remote services totally transparently.

The basis of the Service Architecture is the adoption and implementation of international and industry standards for intercommunication over networks. This architecture will address the means of service connection across the network and provide the basis for providing value added and pan European services.

3.  The **Server Architecture** addresses the strategic objectives of Supplier Independence and Local Information Processing. It describes the hardware and operating system environments within which the applications and services will be developed and used. It comprises technology platforms for corporate computing (currently VME), personal computing (currently MSDOS) and departmental computing, UNIX.

4.  The **Application Architecture** addresses the strategic objectives of Application Portability, Local Information Processing, Data Strategy and Operability. It defines the standards and techniques to be used in the analysis, design and implementation of systems for all the technology platforms defined in the server architecture. It defines the data analysis methodology, the data management systems, training techniques and product tool sets to be used in building common application environments. For the UNIX technology platform this is X/Open.

5.  The **User Interface Architecture** addresses the strategy objectives of a standard User Interface, Growth, Security and Operability. It defines the standards for the use of presentation products and the structure and composition of the user presentation menus. Its goal is to provide a standard user presentation interface in terms of screen and keyboard interactions throughout the AA.

6.  The **Security Architecture** provides a framework within which the AA corporate security policy can be implemented. It must provide systems covering data integrity, access control, distribution of data and code, public network access as well as the classification and declassification of data, users and applications.

7.  The **Data Management Architecture** addresses the need for a Data Strategy and as such is intimately related with the Security and Application Architectures. The basis of the architecture is the definition of techniques and facilities for the distribution, security and archiving of data throughout the AA. It also addresses the aspects of user ownership and accountability for data.

That in a nutshell is the Information Systems and Technology strategy for the AA. It is simple, but reflects a consensus, an agreement of the goals to be achieved by the whole management and staff which is considerably more difficult to achieve than simply circulating a document which will be read and filed away.

Some lessons which were learnt and some issues raised are worth serious thought. In early 1987, during the design phase of our X.25 network, a requirement was identified to run a local PC-based application in the high street shop which needed on-line communications to the mainframe data centre. The IS and IT management were in the process of getting their business plan together and an external consultant (supplied free by BT for their own reasons) was brought into IT division to conduct a study of the telecommunications strategy in the AA.

The telecommunications study detailed far more than just a communications strategy, it looked at the types of technology that were being implemented on the network and the operating system and software issues associated with future developments based upon a concept of Open System standards.

This started IT division thinking about technology platforms.

At the same time, the IS development teams were having problems, it seemed the wrong PC had been chosen, not enough store, not enough speed etc. Proprietary protocols had also been chosen to communicate across the network, the old network, not the X.25 one that was coming into being.

Another lesson is to be learnt here. Management Services Group had considerable technical expertise, but in the wrong area, mainframe people were applying their knowledge and techniques to a distributed problem.

At this point IT division floated the first two building blocks of the architecture: the network architecture, which basically used X.25 for wide area connection and 802.3 LANs within the sites, and the server architecture, which used MSDOS on a 286-chipped PC for the workstations and UNIX for the server functions.

These two building blocks gave IT division the opportunity to move into buying commodity products, reducing the all-up cost of the system and future-proofing it in line with the 60 months' target.

There was considerable resistance to the strategy, particularly from those deeply involved in getting their systems developed on time. Their attitude, quite understandably was that IT division were moving the technology goal post every time they reached the half way line of development. The consultant's report was eventually rubbished by IS as being untimely, technically biased and leaning towards a certain supplier.

Management Services split into two distinct camps. This is the point where a second consultant came into play. This one was an external, independant consultant. His role was to act as a facilitator, to explain in plain English the pros and cons of the approach and hopefully heal the split. This consultant was independent, not from the AA and not from any vendor, he was perceived as being no one's man, he had no axe to grind and his measure of success, his fees, were dependent on our success. So through numerous meeting, discussions and presentations, the split started to heal and through his office the other building blocks of the overall architecture were built.

Management Services group had a strategy, a document and consensus, it had in fact evolved over a period of twelve months. The next stage was to implement it and manage it.

Implementing a strategy is really all about educating everyone involved, the staff, the users and even the suppliers.

Managing a strategy, which is a constantly evolving beast, absorbing changes in technology as well as changes in business, requires a management structure to be put in place. An IT review panel was formed, responsible for the overall strategy. Reporting to them are a series of working groups, each responsible for one of the architectural building blocks of the strategy and imposing standards, by testing and approving products and feeding back their findings. R&D project are owned by these groups, thus feeding new knowledge and experience in at the bottom.

All this is now in place and the ball has started to roll, and by doing so has highlighted issues that are not covered by the strategy.

1. Organisational Issues. The power exists to radically change the way the AA does business. But is the organisation prepared for such a dynamic change of climate?

2. Manpower strategy. Management Services group has had to change radically the way it has recruited, trained and organised its staff.

3. Measurement Issues. Although the working groups have realistic and measurable objectives set against them, this process needs to be driven down and down the organisation.

4.  Management of non-conformance. Management Services group is aware that the strategy is an ideal and that there will be occasions where a pragmatic non-strategic solution is the only way to solve the problems, but how is that managed within the framework of the strategy? Growth by acquisition poses a similar problem, how are acquired systems integrated that have not followed a similar strategy? And how can specific industry moves be exploited in sectors like insurance and travel that are not covered by the strategy but are essential to retain competitive advantage?

These are the areas that are currently being addressed.

## THE ISSUES

The strategy must be business driven. It cannot be done in isolation, as it must be built on the back of the long-term business plans. Management Services were unable to formulate a reliable strategy until the business planning process was in place. This has enabled the group to move away from being reactive to using IT proactively in support of competitive advantage.

A strategy is not a piece of paper; it is a consensus of agreement to a set of goals and the means of achieving them. This means to start with, a champion or champions are needed that will drive the formation of the strategy, then the critical mass of management must be won over.

The strategy must be disseminated to everyone. It cannot and must not be seen as an elitist management tool. The strategy is written for the information infrastructure of the organisation; it will impact on everyone, therefore, everyone must know about it and be behind it.

A strategy is a living thing; it is a continually evolving process of assessment and refinement, so that no opportunities are missed in the future.

It will cost time and money to put the strategy together. It took hundreds of management hours plus the cost of external consultants to put the AA's strategy together. It will cost money in terms of reskilling the staff in new areas. But that is an investment the AA is confident will bring the desired returns.

Attempting to change the culture of the management group and their staff away from the safety of their old experience to planning for the future is not a trivial task, and it is not achieved overnight.

## THE BENEFITS

What then are the benefits of taking this approach?

It has given the AA a framework of technology platforms without being dependent upon any one supplier.

It is already starting to reduce costs. The AA has an investment plan; commodity products are bought in a market where the Association's buying power is used to drive down costs and obtain performance-related contracts.

With the architectural platforms in place Management Services Group are in a position to introduce new systems or services swiftly, as they are required, at marginal incremental cost but with maximum added value.

Management Services are now business driven, not technology driven. The strategy is driven by the business planning process not by annual budgets. It has focused our attention on providing business solutions to support the Critical Success Factors of the business plans. It has also provided a number of spin off benefits.

Management Services are now all talking the same language, the language of our business. This may seem a small thing, but in terms of removing iterations in the development process it is vital.

The development of the strategy has acted as a catalyst to change Management Services thinking and planning horizons. Management Services are now looking and planning for the future, within the framework of the strategy. Every development or investment is a positive step towards the overall business goals.

# 9

# OPEN SYSTEMS POLICIES IN THE NHS

*P. J. Bishop*

*Director, the NHS Information Management Centre, Birmingham*

## INTRODUCTION

This paper will describe Open Systems policies which are in place in the National Health Service (NHS) and will give some examples of how they are being implemented in procuring IT products and services.

The UK NHS is described as an environment in which OS policies are important and the role and activities of part of the NHS - the NHS Management Board's Information Management Group (IMG) are discussed. This illustrates how Open Systems issues are being addressed by IMG.

The paper concludes by saying something about NHS policies that are in place for procuring products which conform to OSI Standards.

## THE NHS - AN ENVIRONMENT REQUIRING AN OPEN SYSTEM APPROACH

By any standards the NHS is a very large and complex business, comprising many large and complex organisations attempting to achieve objectives which are often difficult to define with any precision. In England there are nearly 200 Health Districts providing the health care services required in their geographical area, both to those patients in the well over 1,000 hospitals and to those people requiring care in the community.

It is a large employer of staff, most of whom depend on information from a number of sources in order to perform their work. The quality, reliability, accuracy and availability of this information is often critical. Nurses and doctors, other health workers and managers, all require a wide variety of information. There are some 400,000 nurses, 100,000 doctors and other health professionals, 75,000 professional and technical staff, 100,000 administrative and clerical staff, all of whom require access to comprehensive information about the patients or the organisations for whom they are responsible.

For example, nurses need a lot of information about each patient for whom they care, the problems they have, the treatment they require and a host of very individual requirements. Doctors and other health workers need to keep a mass of current and historical information about each patient and about the resources at their disposal. Managers need to know about a complex and often widely distributed organisation such as a health district. They have to achieve their targets within tight budgets when it is often difficult to have meaningful measures of the outputs and outcomes of the health services provided.

The NHS in England is organised in two separate parts.

1.  The Family Practitioner Services - FPS - comprise contractors such as GPs, Dentists, Opticians, Pharmacists, etc.

2.  The Hospital and Community Health Services - HCHS - comprise the 200 or so Health Authorities.

This paper is concerned with the HCHS part of the NHS.

HAs are organised in 14 regions containing between 8 and 22 district HAs and covering a population of between 2 and 5 million. The NHS is unusual as a national organisation in its devolution of authority to the local HA. This gives rise to many differences in the way each HA works.

Each HA is under the direction of a General Manager who is expected to use the staff, buildings, facilities and funds at his disposal to deliver the required Health Services to that HA's part of the population. This results in HAs up and down the country having very different priorities and emphases in the way they invest in support services like Information Management and Information Technology. Hence we have some Health Authorities who are very advanced users in one information system but have not yet considered others. Systems have been obtained from a variety of suppliers; the one chosen for a given HA often being the system which best satisfies the local requirements of the moment. Problems arise when these systems have to be extended or linked with others. Earlier attempts at introducing standard systems or standard hardware in all regions proved unsuccessful in introducing a common system across all regions and districts.

A survey undertaken a few years back revealed that the NHS, although being very dependent on information for its functioning has a lower than expected level of investment in IT.

It showed that present information systems were separately developed, application specific and, although some were fairly modern, they would need replacing by the mid 1990s. It also showed that in all districts hardware had been obtained from a variety of vendors over an extended period; some had been linked over data networks. The programme for replacement would also be over an extended period. Software and databases were similarly separate with some overlaps (normally inconsistent) and many gaps.

This provided a situation where systems cannot be integrated easily (if at all). They are not consistent in design. They are concerned often with supporting only operational activities and do not provide management information. They are not compatible nor easily transferable to another site.

The same review revealed that many HAs had developed views of the improvements they required. IT should be directly usable by health professionals. Information systems should be able to cater for local needs and be responsive to change and they required comprehensive management information to be available irrespective of traditionally separate source systems. In short they wanted interactive, integrated information systems covering all aspects of the Hospital's or HA's business; in particular all matters about the patients.

This sort of wish list implied a major redevelopment programme and a large increase in the level of investment by HAs. HAs would need to make the transition from their present situation to a future one of their choosing, having produced an information and IT strategy. This would map their path from separate application specific systems towards the improved integrated information system of their choice in accordance with local priorities and when they could afford it. The move would be towards better information from better quality systems.

# THE NHS MANAGEMENT BOARD'S INFORMATION MANAGEMENT GROUP

In 1985 the NHS underwent one of its reorganisations with the introduction of General Management. The Secretary of State appointed a board of directors comprising some from private industry and commerce, some from the Government's Health Department and some from the NHS. One from the NHS was a director with responsibility for Planning and IT - Mr M J Fairey. He was to have responsibility for a collection of both DHSS and NHS staff - his Information Management Group (IMG) - who would pursue the NHS Management Board's intentions.

After a period of discussion with a number of interested officers from all parts of the NHS and DHSS, IMG produced a draft document for discussion within the Service. This was called a National Strategic Framework rather than a strategy because of the nature of the NHS as a confederation of semi-autonomous organisations. This draft became a published document in October, 1986 - *A National Strategic Framework for Information Management in the Hospital and Community Health Services*.

The framework comprises three main elements by proposing that Health Authorities should:

1.  produce information and IT strategies in support of their plans for health services;

2.  adopt a minimum set of standards;

3.  provide information required nationally and by the centre.

The IMG's work programme is the centre's contribution to the achievement of this framework and comprises work that is both necessary for HAs and can only, or most usefully, be done centrally.

The programme contains a whole series of projects falling into several distinct groups. One group of projects is aimed at assisting HAs to produce information strategies. This has been done by developing guide-lines for such strategies along with pilot projects which, using structured methodologies, illustrate the production of information strategies from service plans.

Another group of projects is aimed at introducing a minimum set of IT standards which, among other things, include data definitions, a common basic specification and data communication standards.

An important group of projects are those aimed at defining nationally and centrally required information. This covers health service indicators for all aspects of an HAs activities and a specification for centrally required information. To assist HAs implementating these requirements several facilitating projects have been established both to define design, development and project management methodologies and to support management arrangements for HAs collaborating in joint system developments. There are also supporting projects to produce an Information Management and Technology Training strategy, and a project to assess the impact of information technology on HA activities.

In the course of this work the IMG are producing guidelines for

1. investment appraisal

2. procurement

3. information quality audit

4. information use

5. data protection

6. research and development funding

7. application registers.

A part of this work programme is the responsibility of the NHS Information Management Centre in Birmingham, the unit of which the author is director. The unit employs some 15 IT professionals engaged mainly on work concerned with IT Standards, business activity analysis, data and process modelling and technology assessment projects. The two specific work programmes involving the centre address Open System requirements are the Common Basic Specification (CBS) and the Central OSI Team (COSIT).

## The Common Basic Specification (CBS)

It is a logical model of the business activities of a Health Authority together with the data and processes needed to support those activities.

The objective is to produce a complete set of logical models, enabling an increasing degree of automation in the system design and development process. The models will be a sound basis for building and buying application systems which will be compatible regarding the business processes and data.

The CBS will help to address current problems of integration, compatability and consistency. It will lead towards satisfying a HAs need for corporate, linkable and extensible systems.

Progressively, the main parts will be produced in such a way as to fit together into a whole.

When requiring a part of the integrated system, a designer will go to the CBS Library which contains, in electronic form, many volumes of data and process models and a business activity analysis or functional hierarchy. He will obtain those models which relate to the business activities in question and this will form the foundation of his system design. He will build an implementable system to suit his chosen technology environment using, when available, tools and aids to increase productivity. His final product will be a package which will link with others which are based on the CBS. Progressively he will build up the whole set.

The present position with the CBS is as follows:

1.  data model - a final version has been produced for most of the major activities; this now needs to be completed, tested and refined;

2.  business activity analysis - is in draft and is being completed, tested and refined in a number of development projects;

3.  process models - have now been produced for a small number of activities.

The CBS is an intra-NHS Open System concept and is now being discussed in wider international health circles in Europe and the rest of the world.

We envisage that implementation of the CBS in open software regimes such as UNIX will aid further portability of the products. More work is required in this area before it can be said to be a NHS Standard.

## The Central OSI Team's Programme

The Central OSI Team was set up in September 1986 following a study by a firm of technical consultants into the ways in which the NHS could fulfil the government's and NHS's statement of intent in 1984 and 1985 to use OSI. The consultants' company was CAP and their recommendations to set up a central enabling mechanism - this became COSIT - coincided with other related work undertaken in producing the Framework. The remit of COSIT is to provide central support to HAs in developing communication strategies for migrating existing computer networks to an OSI context, and for developing new OSI-based communication infrastructures.

This role became particularly important when, in 1987, the EEC issued the decision (87/95/EEC) that all public bodies (including NHS) in member states should comply with the mandatory requirements of the directive which was to come into effect in February 1988. Article 5 of this legislation requires the mandatory use of IT standards (principally, but not entirely, OSI) as the basis for the exchange of information and data for system interoperability. COSIT worked closely with the NHS Management Board's Procurement Directorate in assisting HAs to be in a position to comply by February 1988.

The objectives of the COSIT strategy for the implementation of OSI in the NHS are:

1.  to survey existing data communications facilities in the NHS;

2.  to support the development of local OSI strategies;

3.  to support OSI-based network implementations;

4.  to raise the level of OSI expertise in the NHS;

5.  to facilitate inter-authority communications.

From September 1986 to June 1988 COSIT, in collaboration with Health Authorities and external specialists, undertook a series of strategic studies. These studies were intended to enable the implementation of OSI networks in a particular Region or District Authority, as well as to provide a model to other Health Authorities in expediting the development of their own strategies and implementation programme for OSI.

One such study was a national survey of data communications facilities in the NHS. This pre-existence of data communications equipment required the development of a strategy for multiplexor migration to OSI.  Other studies examined the strategy, operational and procurement requirements of a regional data communications network and the development of NHS functional standards covering both use and profile definitions.  Another strategic study produced a proposal for a Naming and Addressing Scheme for the NHS network.

Complementing the strategic studies COSIT was concurrently engaged in a range of enabling activities such as monitoring and assisting the continuing development of OSI base and functional standards. This was complemented by liaison with major vendors to ensure the availability of OSI products and investigating the development of multi-vendor interworking prototypes to demonstrate the viability of the use of available OSI products.  COSIT has also provided in-house technical training and information service to facilitate the uptake and use of OSI.

## PROGRESS

There has been considerable progress towards the use of OSI based networks.  All 14 Health Regions in England have developed or are in the process of developing or even implementing communications strategies based on OSI standards.  A typical approach is the provision of a Region-wide X.25 backbone with one or more nodes at each District.  Since February 1988 all LAN implementations costing above 100,000 ECU comply with OSI, with the majority using ISO 8802.3 standards. Throughout Government OSI Profiles (GOSIP) are being used as the basis for Procurement.

COSIT has established several support activities.  A Prototype OSI Network (POSINET) is now in operation at its headquarters in Birmingham and interworking testing with vendors has started.  An OSI standards Database is 'on-line' to Regional and District data communications staff enabling them to access the latest information regarding the status on OSI standards.  A programme for training senior Regional communications specialists to enhance their proficiency in handling OSI matters, scheduled to start in 1989, is at an advanced stage of development.

The NHS Management Board and the Department of Trade have jointly chosen Northampton District as the OSI Demonstrator site in the Health Service. Key areas of this project are concerned with:

1. ward and family doctor requests for laboratory tests and results;

2. information to family doctors about Accident and Emergency attendances and hospital admissions and discharges;

3. integrating operational, financial and management support systems.

To date COSIT has published a number of documents to assist HAs.


## SUMMARY AND CONCLUSIONS

Health Authorities in the NHS can benefit from developing and implementing their information and IT strategies in an Open Systems environment. The NHS currently uses Information Technology products from all the major manufacturers in typically multi-vendor situations. This is likely to continue into the 1990s in progressively implementing integrated information plans across the whole range of each HA's activities. Compliance with a minimum set of standards is essential in this and we will continue to work closely with all major vendors in an effort to match their offerings with our requirements.

# 10

# IMPLEMENTATION OF A VALUE-ADDED NETWORK IN AN OPEN SYSTEMS MARKET ENVIRONMENT

*M. Anstee,*

*Systems Director, Lloyd's Insurance Brokers Committee*

## INTRODUCTION

My objectives in this paper are to:

1. convey the business requirements and objectives of the London Insurance Market Network (LIMNET);

2. identify the problems and opportunities of undertaking such a project in the light of the main participants being trade associations or "membership clubs";

3. chronicle the selection of IBM as our Value Added Network supplier and subsequent developments.

Once this has been completed I would then like to investigate further the role of Value Added Networks and their relationship with Open Systems architectures. Finally, I will debate whether they might become the major catalyst of industry standards.

## THE BUSINESS REQUIREMENT

London Insurance Market is the world's centre for international insurance and it has been that way for 300 years. It started in Edward Lloyd's coffee shop in 1688 and this year celebrated its tercentenary from Richards Rogers' coffee percolator.

Despite the changes in building, we have always been standards conscious.The vast majority of London's business flows from North America and other international business and trading centres around the world.

The Market, because of its commitment to accepting and underwriting high value catastrophe risk exposure from around the world has, for operational purposes, become a sharing Market i.e. one in which a large number of Underwriting companies (or syndicates) take a small percentage of a risk in order to share the load. As part of this sharing the Underwriting Market has found it necessary, for commercial reasons, to centre its accounting and policy services on three member-owned bureaux. These are the Lloyd's Policy Signing Office (LPSO), the Institute of London Underwriters (ILU) and the Policy Signing and Accounting Centre (PSAC). Within the Lloyd's community itself they have formed bureaux for the processing of claims, reflecting the needs of the Marine, Aviation and Non-Marine Underwriting markets.

It can be demonstrated that there has been a degree of economy and financial saving made across the Market by reducing the resource requirements in certain functions. This served the Market well until the last 5 years when through an increased level of systems sophistication in the Market and the attendant requirements for more information and data, much of the duplication of effort, particularly in the area of data capture systems, has resurfaced.

Today we have a Market comprising 250 Lloyd's Insurance Brokers, 450 Lloyd's Syndicates and 180-190 insurance companies. Between them they have some 27 different computer manufacturers' equipment and in excess of 250 separate model numbers. Their levels of system sophistication are equally diverse. The Market requirement is to communicate and share information between this broad hardware base in a way that will provide for a more cost effective and efficient service to our clients.

## A MARKET ENVIRONMENT

But why the network? For this we must go back in time to 1981. At this time there were a number of very bright thinkers employed in the London Market insurance industry, so bright in fact, that they are now all employed within the London Banking community. However, the concept of a Network evolved from this time and the thought of passing information electronically over telephone wires between the participating companies became first an idea, then a perceived solution and finally, a project. But with a Market as diverse and traditional as London, nothing is ever quite as easy as it may appear on the surface.

To understand our approach to networking and our selection process, you need to understand that the Lloyd's Insurance Brokers, all 250, are in direct competition with one another and that much of their differentiation of service is geared to the level of systems sophistication and speed and quality of service they can offer. The LIBC represents these 250 brokers but it is no more than a trade association. Therefore the LIBC cannot either instruct brokers as to what they should do or commit financially on their behalf. It was therefore surprising that in 1986 they employed a full time network team in order to protect the combined Brokers' interest in Network development and gave the brief to that team to ensure that the London Market Network was installed for the benefit of all of their members.

The Underwriters at Lloyd's, known as Syndicates, are represented by their own managing agents. However, in the centre of Lloyd's is its controlling body, the Corporation of Lloyd's. Therefore it fell, to the Corporation to protect the Underwriters' interest in all things network and to be the negotiating party for all Lloyd's Underwriters on network related issues.The Policy Signing and Accounting Centre (PSAC) is a facility owned and paid for by its membership. Therefore although it could be said that they are more than a trade association, they are not in a position to instruct their members. The ILU is a trade association and the equivalent of PSAC with members owning the whole. Because of the representational role of the ILU, it is seen to operate far more as a trade association than anything else.

So there you have it, four bodies — none with the authority to instruct or even force anything upon their Markets — coming together to select a network supplier and to negotiate terms of trade with that supplier. More importantly, it was the first time that the Market had formed such an alliance so there were no ground rules in place.

At the end of 1986 we were in a position where the Lloyd's Insurance Brokers had just employed their fulltime team to carry out an evaluation of networks. The Lloyd's community had just rejected a long term strategic business plan from their Systems Director, which was based upon a networking concept. The ILU were in the first year of a three year systems rewrite and a conversion to IBM equipment. PSAC alone had agreed with their membership to install a Network service for their members based upon IBM Value Added Network. This had been as a result of experience gained over three years of offering single terminal facilities to the user.

The grouping came together to co-operate in the selection of a Value Added Network to be supplied across the whole London Insurance Market. Our technical specification was wide but simple. We had to have a supplier who could accommodate the connection of a great variety of computer equipment, some of which would have minimal communications facilities. We needed a supplier who could provide both Interactive and IE services. Commercially, we were looking for a well capitalised company who had a long term networking objective and control over the development of, and investment in product.

Although faced with a seemingly impossible task, when we now reflect on developments they were probably only four key decision making factors:

1.  PSAC had already chosen IBM;

2.  only IBM had control over product;

3.  both IE and Interactive facilities were required from day one;

4.  75% of the computers within the industry were IBM equipment.


However, without such benefit we carried out a formal Request to Tender and then an Evaluation Analysis of the responses measuring, where possible, the key attributes of each service. Because of our relative inexperience we had identified our selection criteria based primarily upon knowledge gained from our use of internal networks and external bureau services. Despite the potential shortcomings of this approach, we can now see that they were equal to the task in hand and comprehensive enough to differentiate between the strengths and weaknesses of each of the offerings.

Despite all of these obstacles, the London Insurance Market selected IBM as the supplier of the Value Added Network service to the business community in May 1987.

Having agreed the supplier we recognised that our problems were really going to start. How would we get our community to join the network and, more importantly, what were its initial uses to be?

# CONCLUSIONS

In June 1987 the summary of our position was: IBM selected as network supplier to the London Insurance Market; the Network christened LIMNET, but very little defined by way of usage; no programme for the take on of our community.

Where are we today? We have almost 200 physical connections to the network providing access potentially to 450 organisations within the Market. PSAC made a network connection a condition of membership from October 1988. The ILU have informed their members that a connection will be mandatory by the 31 December 1989, and Lloyd's have circulated all Underwriting syndicates informing them that a network connection will be a requirement for processing claims in the Lloyd's market by the end of 1990. The surprising thing is that there have been very few dissenters and very few objections have been raised, and one can now see that the Market like most other user groups was looking for a lead and direction. Once that lead was forthcoming they understood the need and objectives well enough to comply. Physical connections alone are relatively easy but it is the use of the network which will eventually determine whether LIMNET will be either just a network solution or the major business success that London actively seeks.

Applications to date on the network are few in number. Both PSAC and ILU provide accounting information facilities to their memberships. Lloyd's has enquiry facilities available for the managing agents who operate the Syndicates. Brokers have enquiry facilities into the PSAC database.

Interestingly, there is one application that has caught the imagination of the whole Market with regard to the potential of the LIMNET facility. This is a joint project between PSAC and the Lloyd's Brokers. The reason that it had such a successful start is that the outline of the scheme and agreement to the busines s systems proposals was a result of Executive commitment and involvement from the outset. The scheme itself is important because it tackles a number of fundamental network related issues. Firstly, the Brokers' system must now be capable of providing claims advice information to the PSAC central bureau. Secondly, when the Broker visits the PSAC Underwriter or his claims manager, they must have terminal access to that information. More importantly, they will now both sit on the same side of the desk to agree the content of that claims. Traditionally, Brokers have then gone to visit all Underwriters on a risk. With the new scheme once the Leader and Broker have agreed the contents of the advice, that information is broadcast over LIMNET to all following Underwriters on that particular risk. Therefore, we have achieved effective distribution over the network. The Underwriting companies then have a set period in which to make computer responses to the centre on a limited number of options ranging from automatic approval, through more information required, to please come and see me. This has given us Network based authorisation as the Underwriters are now agreeing to payments of money via computer and, more importantly, they have dispensed with the need to see the Underwriter or his documentation other than for specific cases, contentious claims or high values items. This application went live in November 1988, for both batch facility and online interactive data capture. To date the build up has been a predicted, slow, controlled but encouraging with more Brokers and volume coming onto the scheme each week.

Another major use of the network is electronic mail. The IBM product Screenmail is taking off slowly due, unfortunately, to certain limitations within the product itself and lack of office systems interfaces. Nevertheless, the community is beginning to consider electronic messaging and communication as a potential method for conducting business – which in a Market as traditional as ours is encouraging. Already, in excess of 250 personalised or company mailboxes exist on the system.

So what are the conclusions that I would draw from the selection and installation of LIMNET in a 300 year old traditional Market where no one has the authority to dictate change. I think, quite honestly, that these are simple and probably obvious.

1.  The Market, like most user communities, was looking for guidance and leadership. The leadership had to come from their systems community as the solution was technology based.

2.  Although a traditional Market, London has always been opportunist and entrepreneurial. The business community were quick to spot the opportunities provided and therefore business support from the highest level was quickly gained.

3.  The need for the business edge or competitive advantage, ultimately drove the requirement of the business faster than the planned network developments. So the leaders quickly become the led.

When history is written there will probably be a view held that the Market was forced to change its methods because of commercial pressure. However, it is interesting that the London Market was the first to actively consider and install a Value Added Network despite the fact that logistically it was physically closer together than any other.

# VALUE ADDED NETWORKS AND THE STANDARDS DEBATE

I would now like to turn to Open Systems and the standards debate and the role of Value Added Networks and OSI. Open Systems or standards for the same, have been with us for many a year. In fact, I believe it was in 1975 that I was first introduced to a certain manufacturer's **soft machine**. This particular computer was introduced on the basis that it would operate solely on microcode and that its architecture internally was flexible enough to operate in the morning as an IBM 370, in the afternoon as an ICL 2900 and in the evening as an NCR Century. The reason I raise this particular example is that the machine itself was neutral: there was little clear definition of how it would operate in its own native environment. The machine I refer to was the NCR Criterion. Perhaps it was ahead of its time, because apart from the development of the IBM PC and compatible clones we have failed even to encourage or achieve standards across hardware at anything above the component level.

During this conference there has been much discussion on operating software and the visionary future of UNIX-based operating systems across all machines. Unfortunately, I fail to be convinced that a single standard will be achieved in the foreseeable future with UNIX, ZNIX all vying for support.

Moving further up the chain, we come to application software. In my view, as an industry we have failed in the vast majority of instances to provide applications or application development languages that are acceptable across a serious range of machinery. Moreover, the actual application software packages themselves are normally polarised onto particular manufacturers' equipment.

Even when we have achieved a degree of commonality in the software area, we have found that its transportability has been limited because of the peripheral dependencies of its access and data storage architectures.

It is not until we come to communications that we start to find some areas of commonality, but in the area of physical communications we still have a long way to go with regard to modems, coms card, drivers and the like. The communications architecture is well defined, but again we have multiple uses, X.25, OS 400 and SNA all with their own variations. But what about communications applications? Even here the services offered by our Value Added Network suppliers — be they Telecom Gold, IBM Screenmail service, IBM Store and Forward facility or that of INS and ISTEL — are all different.

In all our efforts the one thing we have been singlarly successful at doing is in polarising our communities along specific lines in hardware, operating software, application software, peripheral dependency and communications.

Where is this leading us? Basically, I believe that it is in the standards and the network applications areas that true interconnectivity will exist.

In different Markets we are starting to see transportability both in information and services — which is why I would like to open the debate on Value Added Networks as the prime driver in the Open Systems environment.

Theoretically a Value Added Network is the ultimate Open Systems connectivity link because of the requirement that a Value Added Network should be able to interconnect any business activity. Value Added Networks impose certain disciplines on both the operational software and application software that is developed by the various manufacturers. In our selection of IBM as our Value Added Network supplier it could be said that we gave total disregard for Open Systems philosophy. We would counter argue that IBM probably has the most structured and well designed internationally acceptable architecture in the world. It may not be the best, it may not be open, but at least everybody understands it and manufacturers have been building emulation products and facilities for many a decade.

I would like to divert for a moment or two and look at the way Value Added Networks will ultimately impact system development principles, applications and internal computer systems operations. Firstly, computer systems over the last five to ten years have been built on an ever-increasing philosophy of online interactive data capture. In many instances it has not been seen as necessary to rebuild the old fashioned bulk batch data collection facilities as we have now transfered data collection out to the practitioners or technicians in our companies. Data capture is now part of our way of doing business. It is an integral part of the job. We have always argued the case that practitioners are far more aware of the content of the information and therefore their input will be more accurate. But now, with Value Added Networks, suddenly the potential is there for all or most of the of information will arrive in the old fashioned batch mode over the network link to be fed into existing systems. There can be no online interactive validation, information will also have to be notified of the rejections back over the network.

Within my own environment we are beginning to look carefully at these changes and their impact on the basis we use in deciding what systems will be developed and how they will constructed. The questions we are asking ourselves are listed below.

1.  When will emphasis be placed upon database structures that allow batch update and interactive enquiry ?

2.  Will each party need to hold as much information as he does today? Particularly as he may be able to equire on his trading partners databases.

3.  How much information will need to be held centrally (Market database) compared with that held locally (company) ?

4.  What standards will be required for data exchange, enquiry, security and sign-on etc?

5.  Can programme functions keys have a standard meaning?

6.  Will $ and £ transmit correctly or will all currencies have to be represented by the ISO Standards of GBP and USD?

The reason I raise these issues is that we are about to witness a change in trading patterns that will be reflected throughout the systems environment. There will be printing and more communications, external communications for internal terminals, peer-to-peer coupling and low-volume online access from many external sources. There will be more sophisticated search facilities and window techniques, far more PC LAN links to hosts which may well become pure data drivers, sophisticated but easy to use comms facilities that can incorporate industry standards packages (INTERBRIDGE) and reflect international standards (EDIFACT). We might even see standard application packages being installed across whole Market sectors.

These are exciting times for business and for standards and I would make one small plea on behalf of my business community to the manufacturers and suppliers to our industry. It is this: if we are going to move towards a set of standards for operating systems and comms protocols then please let us have only one set!

# 11

# ELECTRONIC DATA INTERCHANGE: BRITISH COAL AND THE EDICT SYSTEM

*W. L. Bedford*

*Chairman, EDI Steering Group, British Coal*

## THE COMMERCIAL APPLICATION OF EDI

The following are some quotations from EDI experts and market leaders:

A dramatic change in business practice is now taking place not only in the UK but across Europe and throughout the rest of the world. Coupled with the creation of truly free European Market in 1992 it will put massive demands on the creativity and innovation of business management. This change is called EDI (Electronic Data Interchange).

Electronic Data Interchange is already revolutionising the world of international trade. Existing communication tools such as the telephone, facsimile, telex or electronic mail will no longer be sufficient to maintain a competitive edge. Those companies without the new technology may find themselves at a severe disadvantage against the dynamic young businesses who embrace electronic data interchange as part of their corporate culture. Similarly, the advent of the single European Market in 1992, opening up the British Market to even sterner competition, has grave implications for those businesses that do not plan for the commercial realities of the future.

Doing business without electronic data interchange will soon be like doing business without the telephone.

When I walk around my warehouse I can normally tell which suppliers are using electronic data interchange - those that have much lower stocks and delivered to my requirements without any problems.

British Coal are committed to electronic data interchange. In due course the use of electronic data interchange will be a requisite for trading with British Coal in many business areas.

Overall, companies have no option but to resort to EDI at some point. Management might as well start thinking in EDI terms now - and consequently help to shape its policy - rather than be forced to adopt EDI later.

## What, then, is EDI?

EDI is the computer to computer exchange of business information electronically between business parties (and possibly intermediaries) in a structured format. Because of the structured format electronic documents can quickly be transmitted from one computer system to another without manual re-keying the information. In short it is paperless trade.

Growing interest in EDI is evidenced by the rapidly rising numbers of EDI seminars, conferences, published materials, news releases, consultants and vendors. The purpose of this presentation is to explain the practical commercial application of electronic data interchange and bring out the consequential standards issues. It is important to stress that EDI is not in itself a technology; it is purely a good business practice taking advantage of technology that has been around for a number of years.

## The Business Problem

The climate from which electronic data interchange emerged can best be described as the paper chase. For many years companies of all types have been using computers to process and then print information much of which is passed to distributors or suppliers by post or even telex and telephone. This information takes the form of orders, invoices, price lists, remittance advices, statements and finally payment. In many instances this information has to be re-input into a computer for further processing. The cost and delays inherent in this process and contribute significant amounts both directly and indirectly to company overheads. Many of these overheads however, are eliminated by transferring the information directly from computer to computer - electronic data interchange.

With the advent of electronic trading the paper-based approach has been clearly shown to be slow due to physical transportation constraints and the delays incurred in the handling of internal and external mail. The transcription and keying processes are notably error-prone which lead to costly mistakes and consequential remedial action. The lack of control over the documentation from the sender to the recipient is also a matter of concern with no guarantees of a safe delivery. Last but not least, the whole paper-based trading process is expensive with estimates of around £10 per document commonplace. It is an established statistic that 70% if any computer's input originates from the output of another computer system.

To illustrate how this problem can be tackled I propose to give a short case study on my organisation, British Coal, for which I am the controller of EDI activities.

## BRITISH COAL

### Computing Base

Mining today is a high technology, high productivity industry which makes use of computer technology all the way from the coal face to the surface and across the whole range of our internal business. Computer systems have been developed using the latest technology for over 25 years, commencing when the industry employed over half a million men at 500 collieries.

British Coal primarily use DEC and IBM equipment. The DEC equipment operates at collieries in a technical environment and is engaged mainly on the remote control and monitoring of equipment underground back to a central control room located on the colliery surface. The IBM equipment comprises a network of mainframes located at purpose built computer centres within the major coalfields, eight distributed processors at Area offices and over 4,000 terminal devices linked into this network, There is also an external services bureau called Compower operating from the mainframe sites plus several franchise offices. The two major centres are at Cannock and Doncaster.

The Corporation wish to develop the use of the computing capability to strengthen links with trading partners to make it easier for them to do business. The coal industry has always been at the leading edge of computing in its commercial activities and its in-house stock control and purchasing system, processed at the Cannock Computer Centre, is acknowledged as one of the most advanced in Europe. On-line data capture and updating of information allied to highly sophisticated stock control techniques has been carried out for many years to keep data for business and management decisions as current as possible.

British Coal have found that suppliers progressively increase their computing capability to handle this business but the link between businesses has relied on the clerical operation of putting orders and invoices into envelopes, sending them through the post, and then requiring a manual keying operation before the data is actually held by the recipient computer for further action.

## Key Statistics

In 1987/8 British Coal had a turnover of £4.4 billion, with an annual spend on goods and services of £1.3 billion. The purchasing function, centralised on the Doncaster Headquarters, but with delegated responsibilities in each of the Corporation's Areas, provides a service to 94 collieries and 13 central workshops. Each pit has its own stores facility which is supported by a network of nine central warehouses. The Corporation actively trade with about 12,000 suppliers, although 80% of all purchases are made from some 2,500 suppliers on nationally negotiated contracts. Current stock value is approximately £165 million, representing 200,000 different items stocked.

The computer systems to handle the purchasing and stock control functions are based on a mainframe computer located at Cannock, with access through over 400 terminals at some 150 locations from Headquarters to pit level. They generate in excess of 500,000 orders per annum.

On the invoice side, British Coal have recently centralised all invoice processing at one location. Now, over 1.8 million invoices are received a year by the Corporation's Suppliers Accounts Department at Doncaster. Existing computer systems enable Suppliers Accounts to input invoices against stock orders or direct purchase orders and where there is a match against price and quantity, automatically generate payment. Over 80% of stock invoices and 65% of direct purchase invoices are automatically matched successfully.

## The Emergence of EDI

The Corporation have thus developed some relatively sophisticated computer systems to handle the purchasing and stock control requirements of the industry. Moreover, the invoice matching facilities available have enabled the elimination of considerable manual effort. Both these activities are processed on central mainframe computers. However, with the volumes involved, the generation of paper orders and receipt of paper invoices represents a major bottle-neck. The wider application, incorporating British Coal's suppliers within electronic networking techniques already established in its own internal activities, was seen as an opportunity to reduce overheads and improve productivity. The coal industry thus became an early pioneer in the introduction of electronic trading.

In 1982, a scheme to prove the techniques involved in electronic trading and gain experience helped in evaluating the potential benefits of creating a closer business relationship between trading partners from the ability to converse electronically. Direct computer-to-computer links with twelve of British Coal's leading mining machinery manufacturers were established to exchange primarily orders and invoices and, in some cases, lead times, prices and lists of critical spares, but in each case it involved a dedicated transmission slot for each supplier to the main computer. Eleven suppliers receive orders, and seven suppliers transmit invoices over direct links and these links account for 14% of all orders and 4% of all invoices by volume. This success prompted a decision to expand the service to embrace as many suppliers as possible.

## Selection of the Network

This decision to expand necessitated the setting up of an interchange system based on the emerging clearing house principle. This was because the majority of suppliers have considerable trading with other companies and need the ability to exchange data over a wide spectrum; it would not be economic to have a dedicated link to each of a huge number of companies and they would need flexibility.

In 1985 a working group with representatives from Finance, Purchasing and Stores, Marketing and Information Technology Departments was formed. In-depth discussions with the then five leading providers of electronic data interchange clearing house technology were held. During this period a survey amongst suppliers was carried out to seek their opinions. The survey showed that a number of companies had heard of electronic data interchange, had computer systems of their own, and were willing to participate with British Coal. Others who had no previous knowledge of the electronic trading concept, expressed considerable interest in following this route. A large number of suppliers to British Coal are relatively small organisations who have little or no computing capabilities; therefore a service was selected that was not only reliable but had a low cost in setting up and subsequent operational running.

In the Autumn of 1986, following detailed investigations into the various EDI alternatives, tenders were invited for the provision of and electronic data interchange service from two companies, namely Istel (EDICT) and ICL (TRADANET - now operated by INS). After consideration of each service against various criteria, Istel were awarded a contract for a pilot service to last two months which, after its successful completion, was extended into a full five year contract.

## CHARACTERISTICS OF EDI WITH BRITISH COAL

### Documents

Initially the EDI project has been driven very much in the context of purchase orders and invoices only. The view was taken that this area alone represented a significant volume of manual work within the industry and was therefore worth concentrating upon. Since then other documents associated with the provisioning and payment functions have been identified which will be advantageous to develop. The development of electronic links with customers is being considered.

### Standards

Consideration was given to the imposition of British Coal's document standards, as used with direct links, on suppliers who wish to trade electronically with British Coal. This was rejected on the basis that, as EDI was expected to grow within the UK, the use of British Coal standards could restrict the size of community prepared to trade electronically with the industry. It was therefore agreed to adopt existing standards but on the proviso that they were sufficiently flexible to cater for British Coal's requirements. The standards bodies operating then were the Article Number Association (ANA) and the Society of Motor Manufacturers and Traders (SMMT) who provided the Tradacoms and Odette standards respectively. There was no universally recognised standard at the time so, by examining British Coal's document content of orders and invoices in conjunction with the formats available from these two bodies the Odette standard for invoices and the Tradacoms standard for orders have since been adopted. Currently, under the auspices of the United Nations, work is progressing rapidly to provide international standards for document interchange. This is called EDI for Administration, Commerce and Transport (EDIFACT) and British Coal is monitoring its progress with a view to adopting this approach as the formats receive wider acceptance.

## Costs

In addition to the five year contract sum of £20,000, British Coal have estimated that a further development cost of £50,000 will be required. This represents the system development work required plus the man hours devoted to liaising with suppliers and assisting them with the establishment of electronic links. The expenditure is of this magnitude because British Coal are adopting a driving role in their industry sector, but for the vast majority of companies the costs are significantly less. For the supplier, the basic fee for a three year contract is about £2,000, on top of which an annual subscription of £350 for links to British Coal only, or £950 for links to other suppliers/customers is payable. The estimated costs of the actual system usage are small on the basis that 75 transactions can be sent for the cost of a 10p telephone call. For the majority of suppliers these costs are acceptable.

## IMPLEMENTATION

The successful implementation of EDI has required commitment from the senior management of a number of departments within British Coal. To ensure effective liaison and co-ordination during the development of the project, a Steering Group was established with representatives from each of the functions involved, including Information Technology, Purchasing and Stores, Finance and Marketing and the Compower bureau.

As already mentioned, before making a commitment to the EDICT service a two-month pilot was run with two of British Coal's suppliers who were already subscribers to the Istel service. The decision to proceed with the full EDI service was taken after successful completion of the trial in February, 1987.

The initial stage of the implementation programme involved the identification of the main suppliers by volume of orders and invoices to British Coal. These firms were invited to a series of seminars run jointly by the Corporation and Istel at which the case for EDI and British Coal's commitment to the project were put forward.

After each seminar suppliers were approached in turn to encourage them to make the commitment to EDI. This involved contact by Istel themselves supported where necessary by systems development staff to handle any technical queries, and commercial staff to emphasise commitment to the profect and the potential commercial benefits that could be accrued.

A series of seminars have been held where some 300 suppliers have been approached. These represented the companies with whom the volume of paper flow was such that substantial benefits could be derived from electronic trading.

To date 125 suppliers are committed to electronic trading with British Coal, representing one of the largest communities of electronically connected companies in Western Europe. Additionally, over 20 companies have verbally committed to using the service in the near future; their only delaying factor is the computer system development work they are currently undertaking to get into shape to communicate with other companies. In fact, half the Corporation's top 100 suppliers receive orders and send their invoices electronically. Of the remainder, about 60 firms originally rejected EDI outright and the rest have all indicated a willingness to consider EDI but are not in a position to develop electronic links immediately. The phrase "originally rejected EDI" was used because some of these companies have since decided to re-consider their position. This is a good indication of increased EDI awareness. Of those who have signed, 70 firms are currently receiving electronic orders in some form and 45 are transmitting invoices; the remainder are at the preparation stage. These represent 24% of all orders and 9% of all invoices. As an indication of progress being made, these figures are changing each week.

The British Coal suppliers who have so far joined the EDICT network represent a wide cross-section of firms. Although general engineering firms predominate, electrical equipment manufacturers, chemical suppliers and stockist/distributors of various commodities have all subscribed. The size of the firm has also been varied, from some with a turnover of under £0.5m to firms with a turnover in excess of £500m.

On average it has taken about twelve weeks from a supplier signing an agreement with ISTEL to actually transmitting live data (although one supplier reduced this to 1.5 days by using a PC software package). A contributory factor to the delay is the software development needed to enable the capture and transmission of electronic documents. The introduction of EDI is often just one amongst many demands on DP development resources. In anticipation of this and to overcome the difficulty, British Coal, using its external bureau Compower, have developed low cost PC packages (i.e. less than £200) for data capture and data entry. With a standard PC and modem, a supplier is thus able to plug into the EDICT network. This solution has been adopted by over 50 of the Corporation's suppliers, some as an interim measure, and has allowed them quickly to start receiving and transmitting documents. It has also provided a breathing space in which the more complex problem of mainframe system modifications can be tackled. Two other major industries have commenced discussions with Compower to provide a similar PC software option.

## BENEFITS

There is little doubt that the Electronic Data Interchange has already provided a number of benefits to British Coal:

1.  error free transmissions of documents, avoiding mistakes arising from re-keying;

2.  cost savings as a result of reduced paper handling and keying in of oringinal documents, estimated already at £50,000 per annum;

3.  rapid transmission of documents between the Corporation and suppliers;

4.  reduction in work associated with invoice queries.

However, these savings have merely scratched the surface and as the system becomes fully established the Corporation will be looking to achieve additional savings, including:

1.  shortened delivery cycles and lead times providing stock reductions (potential £3m per annum);

2.  greater control over timings of delivery, of particular significance for "just in time" provisioning of workshops;

3.  reduced purchasing costs as suppliers take advantage of improved cash flow arising from improved payment of invoices plus the benefits of links with their own suppliers;

4.  electronic mailing services with suppliers.

## THE PROBLEMS

Although the benefits are real, there have been some problems associated with the introduction of EDI that were not fully appreciated at the outset, although some aspects did show on direct linking.

Persuading suppliers to commit themselves to the concept has taken considerable effort on the parts of both the Corporation and Istel. About 25% of the firms approached signed with Istel almost immediately; a corresponding 25-30% rejected EDI outright. The remainder have absorbed many man hours in selling the concept. This has not been because of reluctance to adopt EDI as such, but more because it has represented an additional outlay and additional demand on iternal DP resources. In this respect the British Coal low cost, easy to install, PC package has proved invaluable in helping suppliers to obtain the benefits of EDI much sooner than would otherwise have been. Some companies have, not surprisingly, used delaying tactics in an attemt to create leverage at contract renewal time but Purchasing Officers are alert to this and have developed counter leverages - hence, the number of companies coming back who have suddenly reconsidered their position and wish to proceed.

From an operational point of view the development of electronic orders has proceeded relatively smoothly. The invoice leg has, however, been more problematic. Where fixed payment terms (e.g. net monthly account) have applied, and no advantage could be gained from accelerated transmission of invoices, suppliers have perceived little benefit from the transmission of invoices and have not therefore been as committed to its development. Moreover, acceptance of invoices into the British Coal computer has required a high degree of accuracy from the invoice generated by the supplier. Unfortunately many telephone orders are placed on suppliers and often full details of order number, location code etc. are not picked up and therefore not recorded on invoices, resulting in their rejection. An enhancement to the EDI link which will generate automatic invoice mismatch reports for the supplier is being developed. This is hoped to overcome these problems as it will automatically let a supplier know that an invoice has failed to match, and why. Also, to encourage suppliers to send their invoice electronically the effect of paying by BACS and transmitting the corresponding Remittance Advice via EDI is being examined.

As a means of ensuring that the project develops to its potential Steering Group meetings, at six-weekly intervals, are being held where all relevant matters are aired and action points allocated. The Group is composed of IT staff plus representatives from the commercial user departments within the Corporation who are actively involved with trading partners and can monitor the affect of EDI links and identify areas of development. Istel play a major part in the activities of the Group and British Coal are very satisfied with their performance and commitment.

## THE FUTURE

British Coal are committed to the expansion of electronic trading links. It is envisaged that at some point in the future the use of EDI will be a requisite for trading with British Coal in many business areas.

Having targeted the key suppliers in terms of invoices and orders, attention is being directed at the next tranche of suppliers. The approach now being taken has been slightly modified. Instead of major seminars with 50 or so firms in attendance, small groups of companies from identifiable market sectors are being targeted. It is anticipated that by the end of 1988, 150 British Coal suppliers will have committed themselves to EDI which, by 1989, will have grown to approaching 300. By that time it is expected that between 40 and 50% of all orders and about 25% of invoices will be transmitted electronically.

With the basic infrastructure for orders and invoices established, the Corporation must now ensure that full advantage is taken of the network benefits. Lead times recorded on the stock systems will be reduced by taking advantage of faster communications. Commercial negotiations will seek to recover some of the cost savings being achieved by suppliers. The basic order/invoice links will be enhanced to take advantage of other potential facilities, including invoice status reports, remittance advices, order amendments, order acknowledgements by exception, delivery schedules and advice notes.

Links with suppliers have provided the initial impetus to the development of EDI, but within the next few months links to the Corporation's own customers will be developed. In fact, the top ten customers have been identified and some initial discussions held.

British Coal are also very active in promoting EDI on as wider scale as possible because it is felt that an enlarged community of traders will benefit all. British Coal were represented on the Steering Committee for EDI88, the major EDI event of the year (which was held in early November), and provide information at numerous seminars and conferences on the experience gained in their use of EDI.

Although British Coal have made an initial commitment to Istel, consideration will be given at some point in the future to the community of suppliers growing on the INS Tradanet network. The IT Department of British Coal has been actively encouraging Istel and INS to provide a gateway between the two services so that any user would only require to have one access into both communities. An announcement has just been made that the gateway facility will be available in January 1989, and the Corporation have offered to be one of the pilot organisations to prove the link. Discussions have commenced with British Coal and three of its trading partners to identify the requirements for a pilot.

Finally, as British Coal are moving towards breakeven every avenue of cost cutting and efficiency is being exploited. EDI is regarded as a strategic initiative in this drive. The pioneering phase has been completed and benefits are proven. The Corporation's trading partners are also benefiting by reduced costs and a general increase in overall business efficiency.

EDI development and application experience has reached a state where the question must be, "What is the justification for not operating Electronic Data Interchange?"

## EDI AS A GENERAL SOLUTION

### The solution - Paperless trading

Returning to the general situation on EDI, you can now see that the approach to be taken is to move to computer to computer links. However, as I have outlined there are severe restrictions on a one-to-one basis, not least the possibility that each such link may necessitate generating a personalised set of standards. By operating through an EDI clearing house these issues are resolved for subscribing trading partners.

### Benefits of Paperless trading

There are three areas of benefit which have been proved by the leading practitioners of EDI and take the form of:

1. reduced costs, in terms of clerical effort, paper, postage, and the reduction of errors;

2. improved business practices, getting the right product to the right place at the right time;

3. market advantages and opportunities, being responsive to change, being able to retain valued customers and improving the customer service.

## EDI Today

There are over 1,500 EDI subscribers and this population is growing at the rate of 200% per annum and increasing. Sixty of the *Times* top one hundred companies are using EDI today. EDI is not restricted to any particular profile of user and current practitioners come from all sizes of company, all levels of technological expertise and sophistication. The marketplace for EDI users is completely widespread and publicity is global. The recent event EDI 88, which was the UK's second major annual conference on the subject, attracted nearly 1,400 delegates worldwide.

The types of information being transmitted have no limits and covers the whole spectrum of commercial and technical data. The leading countries in this field are the USA, United Kingdom and Japan who are estimated to be eighteen months ahead of Europe. In fact, comparing the number of companies using EDI to the total number of companies in any particular country, the United Kingdom has achieved the highest percentage of EDI penetration.

The development and promulgation of standards for the interchange of trading data has been ongoing for at least 10 years at various national and international levels. Within the UK, work has to date been done by the Simpler Trade Procedures Board (SITPRO) and the British Standards Institution (BSI) in setting guidelines for people designing messages and setting standards for the data elements used in Electronic Data Interchange. The main principles and much of the detail of these standards has been agreed with the United Nations Economic Commission for Europe and the International Organisation for Standardisation.

The standards currently in use in the UK are those formulated by the ANA and SMMT and the data formats were designed to be independent of transport medium (paper, magnetic tape or transmission line). However, for EDI to become a truly global means of data interchange, a universal language is necessary. To arrive at such a standard the UN/JEDI Group integrated the British and European standards in agreement with the Americans to form the EDIFACT (EDI for Administration, Commerce and Transport) international standard (No. 9735) which will eventually form the basis of all international EDI systems. Most of today's formats are based on the same rules as EDIFACT, so speedy migration will be possible.

A significant announcement made in the last month is the joining of forces of SITPRO and the BSI on 1st January, 1989, to fuse their interest in EDI. The ANA have also announced a close co-operation agreement with SITPRO and so we are seeing an extremely responsible attitude emerging on the standards issue in the UK and that can only be to the benefit of all UK traders.

## The Future

I have talked of the visible advantages brought about by electronic trading and these are very real. Management should now be looking beyond these to exploit the hidden benefits electronic trading will open up. Trading opportunities which did not exist in the old paper world can be identified, with business information now available to be passed almost immediately between trading partners irrespective of geographical boundaries — provided that the major companies take the lead in conforming to internationally recognised standards of data format.

The decision to trade electronically and the degree of subsequent exploitation needs to be taken at Board level due to its ultimate significance - the standards issue is often regarded as plumbing and left to the computer people. The strategic importance of adopting a universal standard must be given precedence over technical expediency.

The growth of EDI will undoubtedly continue and many thousands of users are expected to take advantage of this key business practice in the run-up to 1992. EDI is becoming more and more an integral part of the business strategy of companies and is undoubtedly changing the way we do business.

Of all the benefits of EDI, the two that stand out are the ability to provide increased customer services and the acquirement of a competitive edge in your market. This is one area that the United Kingdom has a significant lead over the rest of Europe and we mean to keep it that way.

# Part Four

# Other Issues in
# Open Systems Development

# 12

# PLANNING FOR INFORMATION RESOURCES CENTRES

*C. Lazou*

*University of London Computer Centre*

## THE COSTS AND BENEFITS OF LARGE SCALE COMPUTERS

With the emergence of many small but variable size computers the relationship between the price of a computer and its performance has become significantly more complex. The perception that small computers provide more performance per pound than large number crunchers has gained so much ground that it has become folklore in computational circles. The reasons for this are manifold, not least because of aggressive marketing by vendors of small computers, but to a great extent also because of the layman's assumption that problems of any size can be linearly scaled up, and are thus amenable to be solved using a multitude of small systems instead of one large state-of-the-art number cruncher. Even if this misconception is not challenged at this instance does the perception of "small is more cost effective" stand up when quantified? When one compares technologies of the same generation one finds that the results are a mixed bag. Let us compare, as an example, the megaflops performance of the Cray X-MP/14se and the IBM AT PC (with a floating point accelerator). Using results from the LINPACK benchmark[1] linearly scaled up, it still requires 5000 PCs costing over $10 million to achieve the performance of the above Cray computer which is valued at around $3 million. On the other hand, for roughly the same price, 1000 SUN 3/160s scaled up should outperform the above Cray even in its own patch of number crunching. The new generation workstations such as the Ardent Titan are reputed to have a performance/price ration of three times that of the Cray X-MP/14se. Thus the "mixed bag" results can be demonstrated using claims and selective examples. More importantly all systems have many other attributes and thus the simple measure of floating point number calculation is not a sufficient indicator of why people buy them and consider them as "good value for money".

Exploring this further, it can be argued that, small machines suffer from inherent capacity limits, are poorly utilized, require the scientist to use his/her valuable time for data management, system maintenance, and also waste time in socialising with vendors in the pre/post purchase activities. It must be recognized however, that most users prefer to work with small systems where possible, and for a good reason. Small systems have user friendly interfaces, whereas the user interface of supercomputers has been until now, sadly neglected. Content sensitive full screen editors, distributed systems and window management, developed for workstations, have been absent and only now are making their appearance in a supercomputer environment. Large job queues, maintained centrally and restrictions imposed in the name of improving utilization of expensive hardware, often result in poor turnround responses and tend to waste the most valuable resources of all - the time of the qualified researcher. As a consequence the timeliness and competiveness of the research in hand is lost. In addition, the limitations of network band width adds to the difficulty of using remote central facilities and in some cases, such as on-line visualization, makes it impractical.

In spite of all this, why are centralised supercomputer centres increasing throughout the developed world?

The simple answer is that supercomputers are of the highest and most pervasive strategic importance. They enable scientists to solve today's problems and to develop the new technology for tomorrow's industry, affecting national employment patterns and national wealth. The success of a new motor car design will determine whether employment in car production will continue in Detroit, USA or Longbridge, England. Similarly with aircraft designs and many other applications[2].

People are becoming aware that only supercomputers can feasibly perform certain complex and crucial simulations in product design. 400 bicycles are cheaper but not equivalent to an aeroplane for crossing the Atlantic. Similarly, one thousand workstations or 5000 IBM PCs, are not equivalent to a supercomputer because they cannot be harnessed to carry out a single task. It is this ability of making its enormous resources available to a single job, that makes a supercomputer a unique facility for solving large problems at the cutting edge of technology. Price/performance comparisons are somewhat irrelevant in this context.

It is clear from above however, that this unique capability is made available at the cost of ease of use; and intelligent workstations as local facilities will continue to provide the main interface between the user and the central computing environment. This paper reports on a strategy of the University of London

Computer Centre, for the synergetic integration of central large scale supercomputing facilities, with workstation and other local mainframes, in a manner intended to maximise the essential but complementary advantages of these systems in a unified user friendly environment.

## HISTORICAL

The demand for powerful computational facilities for research in British Universities became appartent by the mid-sixties[3]. The role of supercomputers as strategic instruments for national security, the armaments industry, scientific and engineering simulations in the whole industrial economy, and their performance characterisation are published in the author's book[2].

Facilities at the University of London Computer Centre (ULCC), epitomize large scale computation in British Universities. ULCC was one of two centres (the other was at the University of Manchester) set up in 1966 for the purpose of providing large scale computation to University researchers. From its inception to the early 1980s it used mainly Control Data equipment. In 1987 it was designated an upgrading its computing power from one CDC 7600 to the equivalent of 23 CDC 7600s within six years.

## CURRENT FACILITIES

As a National Centre for Advanced Research Computing, ULCC provides large-scale computer services to members of the academic community throughout Britain. These services are presently based on a Cray 1S/1000 and a Cray 1S/2200 computer running the Cray Operating System COS, and an Amdahl 5890/300 running the IBM system MVS SP. The two Crays are to be replaced by a Cray X-MP28 in January 1989.

In addition a common user interface for users of the three National Centres providing Academic Research Computing is offered via a VAX Cluster using the VMS Operating System.

Other hardware facilities include:

1. a Masstor automatic file store with a capacity of 110 gigabytes to be replaced by a Storage Teck 4400 ACS - with a capacity of 1200 Gigabytes in Spring 1989;

2. graphics based on a DICOMED D148C monochrome and colour microfilm system (35 mm and 16 mm) as well as 105 mm microfiche;

3. 7 and 9 track magnetic tape units with 6250/1600/800 bpi tape density are attached to the Amdahl;

4. Input at ULCC can be in the form:

   (a) diskette - either 5.25 inch (various formats) or 3.5 inch;

   (b) printed documents - the Kurzweil Intelligent Scanning System is capable of scanning a wide range of printed documents and converting the text into machine readable form on either magnetic tape or diskette;

   (c) terminal access;

   (d) File Transport Protocols(FTP);

   (e) Job Transfer and Manipulation Protocols (JTMP).

5. Output to:

   (a) 132 column continuous line printer paper;

   (b) diskette, 5.25 inch Acorn BBC and 360K DOS and PC DOS formats and 3.5 inch Acorn BBC and Apple Macitosh formats;

   (c) Linotronic 300 phototypesetter via the PostScript page description language;

   (d) graphical output in monochrome and colour on 16 mm and 35 mm film and microfiche of various formats of up to 270 pages per fiche are also available.

## NETWORK ACCESS

The majority of jobs enter the ULCC system after being submitted as batch jobs from computers situated in users institutions, via packet switched networks, or direct lines. Both batch and keyboard terminal access at ULCC is provided over a Joint Academic Network (JANET) and the London Networks based on X.25, X.29 and standard coloured book protocols JTMP and FTP. These were developed by the British Universities, in conformity with the ISO model of Open System Interconnection (OSI). Figure 12.1 gives a schematic representation of the ULCC configuration. Figure 12.2 gives a more detailed representation of the Network switches of the configuration.

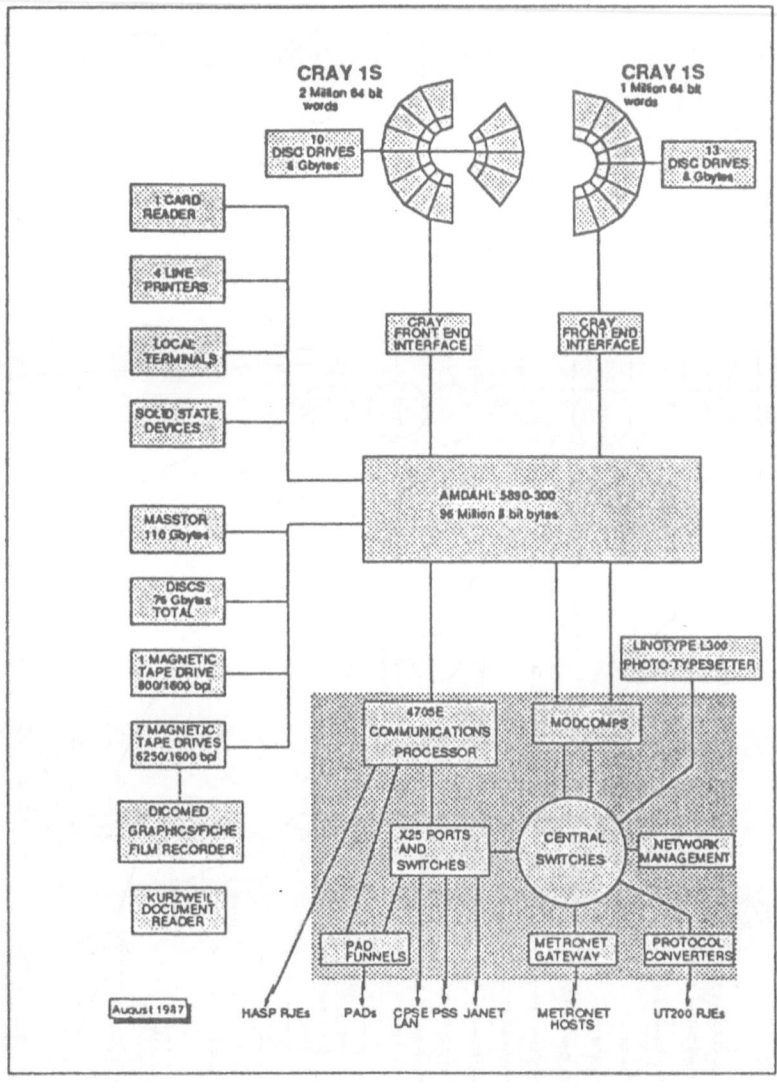

Figure 12.1: ULCC configuration.

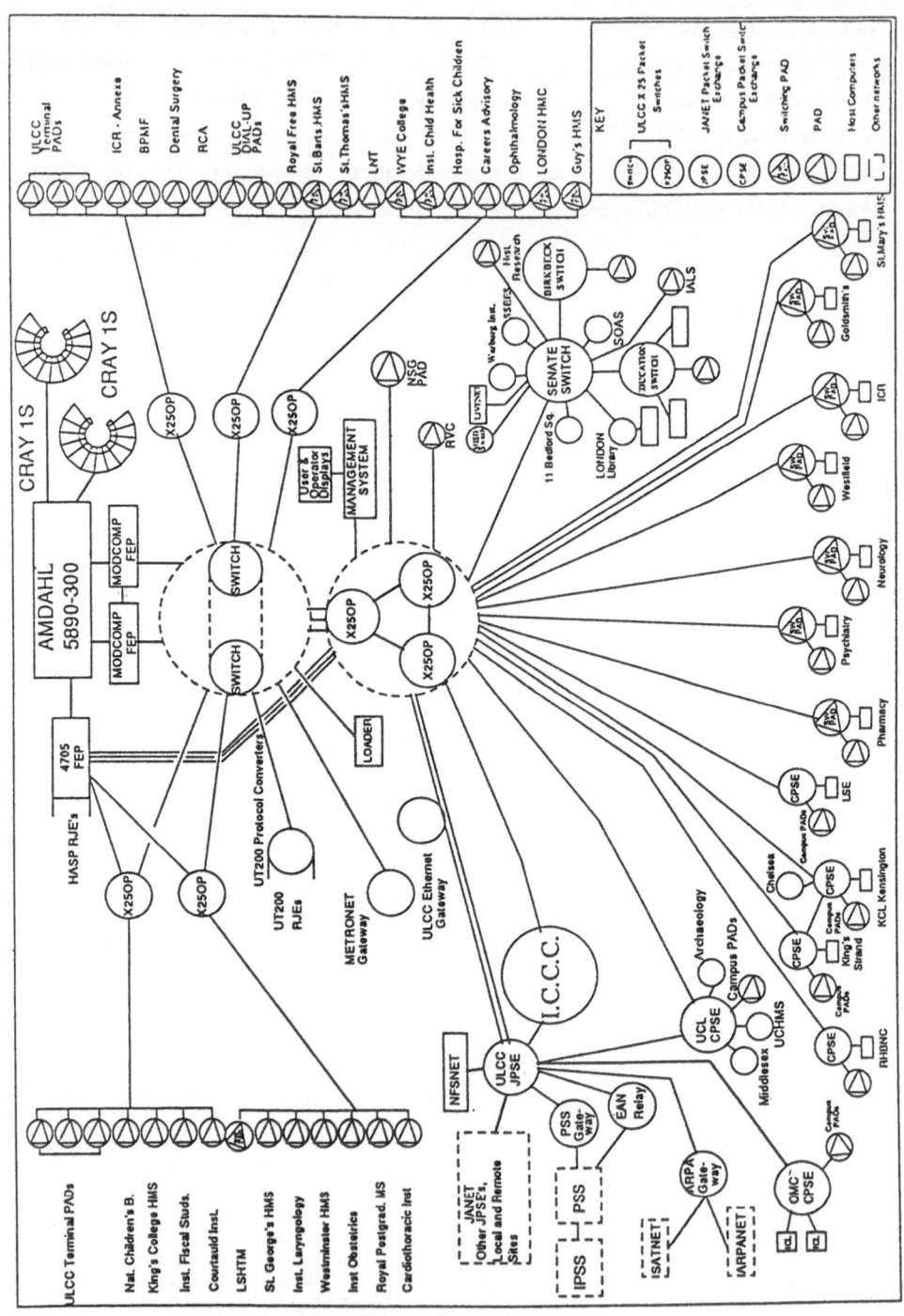

Figure 12.2: Network switches of the configuration.

## USAGE OF THE ULCC FACILITY

ULCC has a user population of about 4500, of that 1200 use the two Crays for Advanced Research computing. The users are mainly research workers in Universities and other higher education institutions. For many years allocation of resources was made on a regional basis to the Universities rather than to particular projects. Since August 1987 the allocation was changed to encompass the Forty [4] recommendations. This new procedure is common to all three National Supercomputer Centres. Briefly, resources are allocated in four sectors as follows:

1. Fully Peer-reviewed sector (Class 1)

> The majority of the Centre's resources (between 55 and 65%) is allocated to this sector. Individual allocations are made by Research Councils and the British Academy after a full peer review and at no cost to Universities.

2. Pump-priming Sector (Class 2)

> This sector is apportioned up to 5% of the Centre's resources for users' pilot projects. Small allocations of up to 0.1% of capacity for periods of up to 3 months are made by the ULCC Director at no charge to Universities.

3. University Sector (Class 3)

> This comprises up to 20% of the Centre's capacity and is for small or beginning users. Individual allocations may not exceed 0.1% of total resources. Universities and other institutions are invited on behalf of their users to take part in an annual round of bids for resources in this sector.

4. Externally supported sector (Class 4)

> Up to 10% of the Centre's resources may be used by academic projects with external (e.g. industrial) support. A charge is normally levied for this sector. Statistics collected by ULCC over a period of years show that on the Crays the dominant disciplines are physical sciences;

chemistry, phusics, mathematics, engineering, molecular modelling, meteorology and oceanograhy; which between them account for about 90% of the total Cray resources. A characteristic of the use of ULCC macines is the broad spectrum of applications. There are for example 79 peer review projects at present with a maximum use of 8% for the largest project. This is in sharp contrast to many other sites where single applications consume high proportions of the supercomputer resources. Figure 12.3 shows Cray usages by department.

The Amdahl resouce is used mostly by University teachers in social sciences and medicine. The dominant use is databases and statistical work.

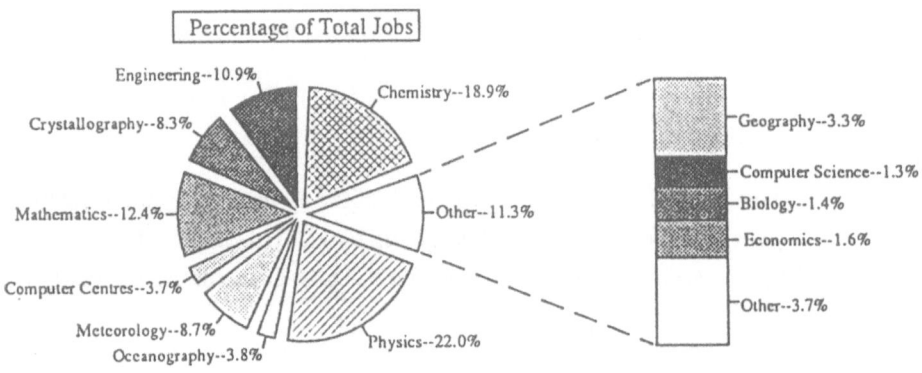

Figure 12.3: Cray - usage by department.

## USER SERVICES

Centralised supercomputer resources pose unique challenges both for users and user services. The advisors and documentation staff at a supercomputer centre like ULCC, face the usual set or requests for hardware status reports, trouble shooting help, and advice on system software. With three major Operating Systems, fourteen languages and seventy five application packages one would have thought this was sufficient. But they also work in a computing environment with five additional special characteristics:

1. frequent technical innovation;

2. strong optimization concerns;

3. collaborative projects;

4. geographically dispersed users;

5. a transient user population.

Each of these characteristics generates extra demands for user support. To fulfill their mission in providing facilities to solve problems at the cutting edge of technology, supercomputer centres need to upgrade their systems every 2-3 years. Often this implies some code conversion for the user. In order to exploit supercomputer features frequent upgrades to the Operating System, Compilers and Libraries are also required. This generates extra work for advisers and for alteration of documents. Apart from regular documents and advice over the telephone a number of other methods had to be adopted. Educational courses for the use of particular elements of ULCC's facilities are provided and in addition advisors meetings are held regularly to familiarise advisors at local institutions with the evolutionary changes of our services. Open user forums for large scale computer users are also held periodically. The use of Electronic mail and on-line documentation has helped to overcome some of the problems of geographic dispersal. The transitory state of post graduate students necessitates that courses must be repeated to accommodate the new batch of users entering the system every year.

Another area which is unique to supercomputer centres is optimization concerns. Despite the rapid increase of the speed with which supercomputers can solve problems it is generally agreed that three orders of magnitude of extra computational power is required to solve some of the pressing problems in fluid dynamics. This pressure to squeeze the maximum performance out of an existing system translates into a further demand on the centre's staff to help users to optimize their codes to effectively use the current computer's resources. Advice on timing techniques for identifying the most expensive portion of the code, on language features and programming techniques that assist vectorization and more recently parallelising techniques for multiple processors (multitasking) become key consulting services. The introduction of industrial partners in collaborative projects with academics provides yet another set of users with their own special requirements and problems for the user services to overcome.

# COLLABORATIVE PROJECTS

Apart from individual codes and application packages supported by ULCC staff, there is a third category of applications. These applications run on the Crays, include protein crystallography, aerodynamics, fusion plasmas, solid state theory, lattice gauge theory, finite element analysis, and are co-ordinated through Collaborative Computational Projects. These are administered by specialist working parties or by the SERC laboratories at Daresbury and Chilton. Staff with post doctoral experience in the particular fields of study are required at the supercomputer centre to interface with users and provide specialist support in these areas. The consultant requires expertise, not only in the effective use of the computer system which service is provided, but also familiarity with the developments of new algorithms in the field.

# FUNCTION ORIENTED SERVICES

ULCC can be perceived as having several functions; namely, to support users of the National service, to support large scale users in London and to support a group of University of London institutions as a ULCC consortium. Users can also be perceived as performing different functions; those of software development and those of production. It is perhaps useful to look at some of the different requirements of these two functions of computer users.

1.  The developer has the following requirements:

    (a)  interactive access with fast response;

    (b)  a functionally broad, and friendly user inteface;

    (c)  debugging tools;

    (d)  visualization facilities;

    (e)  extensive software libraries.

2.  The production problem solver needs are:

    (a)  large amounts of computer resources, primarily in batch mode;

    (b)  high performance using vector of parallel computation constructs;

(c) a stable environment;

(d) simple, functionally narrow user interface;

(e) simple access to (compatible) data and libraries.

Although some of the development can be done on local departmental facilities the process of developing applications specifically for vector architecture must of necessity be done on the supercomputers.

## A ULCC DEVELOPMENT STRATEGY

A development strategy will be guided by the need to provide users within the ULCC functions the following types of services:

1.  leading edge, high performance computational facilities in a production mode;

2.  leading edge hardware in an experimental mode, to allow users to gain experience in the use of new, and sometimes radical computer architectures; before they become practical for production;

3.  other specialised hardware in support of high performance computation, e.g. facilities for graphical visualization and large scale archived storage;

4.  software, educational and advisory support for fostering the productive use of ULCC facilities;

5.  develop facilities and services for establishing a synergetic team work with users, workstations, and other facilities at local universities and departments.

The latter requirement implies the need for uniform network services. The development of standards in the Network area to include user interfaces are awaited with interest. This still leaves the heterogeneous environments presented by diferent operating systems with different editing and submission paradigms. This is a major obstacle which often requires the user not only to use of various network facilities. Many users are unwilling to expend their valuable time in this fashion.

The policy decisions are already in place for the provision of a common user interface for the three national centres. The emergence of UNIX as a de facto standard for Operating Systems and the active standardization process presently with its derivative POSIX, provides a path to overcome the problems emanating from heterogeneous environments. ULCC is committed to migrate to UNICOS on the Cray X-MP28 and the eventual move to a distributed service network where all services are available to all other services. Eventually service modules can be distributed with respect to hardware, software and geography. It is apparent that service connections based on standard network facilities greatly reduce vendor dependence.

Current developments in Open Systems architectures and in data processing standards allows ULCC to contemplate the introduction of object oriented interactive graphics applications running on the Cray, utilizing the capabilities of the local workstation as a visualization service.

In order that this strategy succeeds an ambitious national funding programme has to be established to put the missing hardware in place. Although considerable effort will be needed, in developing the capability and in coordinating its use, ULCC can be playing a leading role for implementing this strategy. In the authors opinion this approach is crucial for the successful propulsion of national services into the computer environments of the 1990s.

## REFERENCES

1.  Dongarra J., *Performance of Various Computers Using Standard Linear Equations Software in a FORTRAN Environment,* Argonne National Laboratory Technical Memorandum No. 23, Edition August 29, 1988.

2.  Lazou, C. (1986) *Supercomputers and their Use* a book published by Oxford University Press 1986. ISBN 0-19-853720-4. Revised Edition 1988. ISBN 0-19-853795-X(pbk).

3.  Flowers, B. (1965) *Report of a Joint Working Group on Computers for Research,* HMSO Cmnd 2883 (1965).

4.  Forty, A.J. (1985) *Future facilities for advanced research computing,* Joint Working Party report (Chairman Prof. A.J. Forty) for Advisory Board for the Research Councils, Computer Board for Universities and Research Councils, Universities Grants Committee, June 1985 Dept. of Education and Science, Elizabeth House, London.

# 13

# STANDARDS FOR SCIENTIFIC LANGUAGES AND LIBRARY MODULES

*S. Hammarling*

*Numerical Algorithms Group Ltd*

## INTRODUCTION

This short paper is concerned with standards for scientific languages and library modules from the point of view of an organization developing scientific software. The author represents a company that develops, markets and distributes numerical and statistical software, but the paper is intended to be relevant to any organization involved with scientific software.

The paper is not concerned with internal company standards, as important as they are, but with external standards and why they are important.

I shall first discuus why language standards are important, and look in particular at Fortran and Ada. Then I shall look at standards for library modules by which I mean components performing basic mathematical operations.

## LANGUAGE STANDARDS

There are a number of reasons for requiring language standards. The most important is probably to allow the development of portable software and hence the ready movement of software between different machine environments. Many man months, even years, can be saved in porting complex systems if the software has been written using an accepted language standards. Writing portable software allows re-use of software components, and considerably reduces maintenance and implementation costs.

Language standards also allow the development and use of standard tools and environments for software development. For example, the Numerical Algorithms Group (NAG) were involved in a collaborative project to develop a set of tools for Fortran 77 programmers, called Toolpack [Cowell, Hague and Iles, 1986], and this is now an integral and essential part of the Fortran software development and processing cycle.

The use of a language standard gives a stable environment for scientific programmers and for the education of scientific programmers, as well as giving the potential for the stable development of language features and facilities. A language standard can even be an important means of international communication.

We should like to encourage European involvement in language standards through participation in the standardization process, the imposition of standards and the funding of standards activities.

# FORTRAN

Fortran is the traditional language for scientific computation and dates back to the 1950s. The standardization of Fortran has been undertaken on behalf of the International Standards Organization (ISO) by a subgroup of the American National Standards Institute (ANSI), called X3J3. The first standard was Fortran 66, the current standard is Fortran 77 [ANSI,1978] and work is nearing completion on the next Fortran standard.

Essentially, Fortran 66 was a subset of Fortran 77, which in itself planned to be a subset of the next standard. Thus there is a continuing steady, stable evolution of the language.

To illustrate the importance of the standard to an organization like NAG, the latest version of the NAG Fortran Library, Mark 13, contains some 1/4 million lines of source code, together with nearly 1/4 million further lines of code for the example and test programs. The Library is implemented on over 70 machine/compiler versions. This would not have been possible without being able to rely on a standard.

# ADA

Ada is of course a much newer language than Fortran, the first standard having been issued in January 1983 [ANSI, 1983]. Ada is also in many ways a richer language than Fortran 77, with features, such as generics, that give even greater scope for re-use of software components.

NAG have been involved early in Ada developments, having received funds from the CEC for collaborative projects in Ada, including a project for a pilot implementation in Ada of numerical software components. The first release of the NAG Ada Library was in 1988.

This experience has highlighted the possibilities for software re-use, but has also shown the need for further standardization. For example, the elementary functions are not defined in the current Ada standard and this needs careful consideration and collaboration, to obtain an internationally acceptable specification.

## STANDARDS FOR LIBRARY MODULES

One aspect of the standardization of software components has been mentioned in the previous section: the need to standardize the basic mathematical operations in Ada in order to gain full re-use of the software via the high level feature of Ada.

A second aspect arises with the advent of modern high-performance computers with architectural features such as hierarchical memory structures and vector and parallel processors. We now have to not only consider software portability, but also obtaining acceptable efficiency when we move software between, or to, such machines.

To achieve this it has been necessary to try and identify a limited number of mathematical operations that from the computationally intense part of as wide a range of algorithms as possible. In particular in the area of numerical linear algebra, this has proved to be feasible and NAG has been involved in two collaborative projects to specify a set of Basic Linear Algebra Subprograms (BLAS) and to encourage these to become de facto standards [Dongarra, Du Croz, Hammarling and Hanson, 1988; Dongarra, Du Croz, Hammarling and Duff, 1988], by promoting international discussion and comment of the scientific programming community. There is strong evidence that this has been successful, and that manufacturers are prepared to provide efficient implementations of the BLAS, so that higher level software utilizing these library modules runs efficiently on such machines.

## CONCLUSIONS

I have discussed the importance of standards to the development of scientific software, particularly the role of standards in the re-use of software components. I believe that standards are vital to the life blood of companies involved in scientific software development, especially as we move to the open market of 1992.

## REFERENCES

1. ANSI, 1978 American National Standard Programming Language, Fortran American National Standards Institute, 1430 Broadway, New York, NY 10018

2. ANSI, 1983 Reference Manual for the Ada Programming Language, American National Standards Institute, 1430 Broadway, New York, NY 10018

3. Cowell, W. R., Hague, S. J., Iles, R. M. J., 1986 Toolpack/1 Release 2 Introductory Guide. The Numerical Algorithms Group Limited.

4. Dongarra, J. J., Du Croz, J., Hammarling, S., Hanson, R. J., 1988, An extended set of Fortran Basic Linear Algebra Subprograms. ACM Trans. Math. Software. 14, 1-32.

5. Dongarra, J. J., Du Croz, J., Hammarling, S., Duff, I., 1988. A set of Level 3 Basic Linear Algebra Subprograms. NAG Technical Report, TR14/88, The Numerical Algorithms Group Limited.

# 14

# DEVELOPMENT AND APPLICATION OF SOFTWARE TOOLS TO VERIFY STANDARDS

*A. T. Twigger*

*Director of Consultancy Unisoft Limited*

## INTRODUCTION

The area of verification and validation is an increasingly wide sphere of activity which is gaining greater importance as demand for Open Systems across differing architectures grows. There has been a noticable increase in interest in software quality assurance and in product conformance over recent months with accreditation procedures being established, branding programmes announced and standards efforts being completed. This paper reviews the requirements for verification in the Open Systems marketplace and outlines some of the principles involved in producing software and providing services to meet these demands.

The context of this paper is based on the author's experiences in generating software for operating system and for compiler verification. There are other areas in which verification is established, in particular networking, in which the same principles have been used to provide verification services.

UniSoft has been involved for five years in the verification field, firstly during the development of the System V Verification Suite and then in the development of the Verification Suite for X/Open (VSX). The author has also been involved in the development of the (POSIX) verification working group.

# VERIFICATION - A HISTORICAL PERSPECTIVE

Historically the computer industry has been beset by the proliferation of proprietary operating systems specifically designed to optimise the hardware capabilities provided by the manufacturer. As technology has progressed, manufacturers have implemented new facilities in their own way, making it increasingly difficult for users to migrate from one architecture to another. This philosophy has generated an abundance of different operating systems and associated procedures in both the commercial and scientific market sectors. The computer user has been faced with a variety of solutions whenever he has specified a problem. Often, the most elegant solution has not been chosen because of incompatibility problems with other computer systems. Occasionally, even manufacturers have faced major problems as technology has advanced and the costs of transition have cut deep against the advantages of the new system.

The standards efforts in the computer industry have, historically, been limited to the area of languages. The production of standards in this area has assisted in the training of development engineers, but has been hindered by the desire of manufacturers to extend the language to interface to their operating system environment. The ability to transfer experienced engineers from one environment to another was restricted by differences in the software generation tools and language extensions. One could always tell whether a contractor really had experience of your system by the number of manuals on his desk at the end of his first morning! The standardisation of languages has failed to produce the increases in productivity necessary for today's needs.

From the standardisation of languages evolved the requirement to verify language conformance for different implementations. This process, undoubtedly, increased consumer confidence in the quality of the language product. For some languages, the verification of a language product was sufficient to guarantee code portability between different environments. In other cases, particularly COBOL, only carefully written code could be transferred from one operating system to another and considerable discipline was required during code generation to ensure portability. In some cases the losses in efficiency through restricting coding practices to a portable subset prohibited the production of portable code.

The results of the years of divergence have been a wastage of effort in training, a wastage of effort in transition of technology, and limitations in the availability of software.

# CHANGING TECHNOLOGY

During the 1980s there has been a dramatic change in computer technology which has brought with it an increasingly perceptive end-user community. The personal computer market has provided a consistency of environment that has allowed the development of software for the mass end-user market. The choices of software packages and hardware are no longer directly related, and in many cases, improvements in technology have been undertaken without major transition costs.

The rate of innovation has also allowed newcomers to establish themselves in the market place with sophisticated technology at a lower cost than would have hitherto been possible. The development of proprietary operating systems has already exceeded the budgets of all but the largest computer manufacturers, and this, coupled with increased market resistance to proprietary solutions, has precipitated the demise of proprietary operating system development. In some cases these newcomers, for example Compaq, have established themselves by taking advantage of a de facto micro-processor based standard. In other cases, for example, Sun Microsystems, the application of Open Systems has provided the platform for success.

The availability of powerful micro-processors has accelerated the move towards standardisation in the operating systems area. Many of the previously critical inefficiencies are now resolved by the increases in processor power availability. Increasingly, the major manufacturers are becoming systems integrators, using industry standard components integrated with both internal and external innovative technology to provide computer solutions for their established user base.

At the same time, the user community's demands are switching from proprietary solutions to an Open Systems philosophy. The end-user sees that Open Systems not only provide a more secure path for the future but also provide a better price performance ratio than the proprietary alternative. The availability of CASE tools and relational database technology is accelerating this move towards the Open Systems philosophy.

# THE CHANGING USER PERSPECTIVE

The end-user perception of their computer requirements is changing rapidly. Fast system prototyping is expected and the development cycle is shortened. Software development needs to be able to address the dynamic needs of a business - no longer can the business be constrained by the data processing resource. The user is looking for a wide choice in available hardware platforms to allow increased flexibility and, possibly, to allow some decentralisation of computer resources.

The costs involved in upgrading to new hardware technology will no longer be tolerated by the end-user community. Backward compatibility will become a requirement, this will become increasingly important as different versions of standards appear and backward compatibility becomes an issue not only with the previous releases from a manufacturer but also with the definitions in previous versions of the standard.

The end-user also expects to see cost reductions and wider availability of packages for horizontal market software. The provision of verified conforming platforms will greatly assist the software developer in achieving cost reductions through increased volumes.

The need to retrain staff when new hardware platforms are introduced should be greatly reduced by the provision of open software. The provision of standard command sets, standard software generation tools and standard operating systems services increases staff flexibility and allows mixed hardware platforms to be readily implemented.

## INDUSTRY'S ANSWER

Open Systems are an accepted reality by all of the major manufacturers in the world. Over one half of the annual computer spend will be applied to Open Systems by the early 1990s.

Considerable progress is being made in producing standards for Open Systems. While much of this work is based on historical implementations, an increasing innovative element is being introduced. The scope of interest in standardisation is widening with both manufacturers and users having the ability to input into the standards process.

The increased pressure to produce a consistent set of standards and for manufacturers to implement to these standards also requires a measure of conformance to be applied. The verification of implementations will become a major issue in the 1990s as the demand for standardisation increases.

In the case of some de facto standards a particular software package has been used as a measure of conformance. While this pragmatic approach has provided some measure of confidence to the user, all to often this informal method of testing has proved inadequate. A more formalised approach to verification is needed to test adherence to formal standards.

## THE VERIFICATION PROCESS

Verification is concerned with the development of, primarily software tools to ascertain whether an implementation meets the standard being verified. In general, standards do not define a measure for conformance and the first step in the verification process is to define this measure. The later steps closely map onto those in a typical software development cycle.

A carefully controlled review process is required to cater for situations where these are either faults in the standard or faults in the verification software. The implementation of a system of waivers is needed to control variances that are considered acceptable. The determining factor in providing a waiver should be the portability of applications onto the platform being tested. If the judgement is that application portability is not impaired, then a waiver can be justified.

## DEVELOPMENT OF ASSERTION LISTS

In order to verify a standard, it is necessary to produce a list of items that are to be tested. Each of the items in this list can be considered as a unit of functionality described in the standard. This process can be considered to be a formalisation of the requirements of the standard and can be used to tighten the definitions contained in the standard. This process requires a degree of paranoia in the approach of the assertion list developer who is persistently trying to generate situations in which the definitions in the standard are untrue.

The assertion writer also needs to be aware of the conditions under which the defined behaviour will occur and to consider any external factors that may effect the implementation of a test.

In cases where a number of different test suites are being developed to verify a particular standard, the final assertion list provides a common denominator that ensures consistency of scope between the different suites. This allows the implementor to retain freedom in the areas of thoroughness of testing and in the test methods chosen.

## THOROUGHNESS OF VERIFICATION

The purpose of a verification suite is to provide a measure of the conformance of an implementation to a standard. While it is theoretically possible to prove conformance, there are many practical issues that prohibit such proof. Therefore, a verification suite can only be used as an indicator of the conformance of a system to the standard being tested.

While a manufacturer may use verification as part of his quality assurance procedure, this can be no substitute for normal quality assurance practices. There are considerable differences between the development methods associated with verification and those associated with quality assurance. In particular, quality assurance procedures can assume knowledge about internal product structures whereas verification must never assume any implementation specifics. Similarly, quality assurance is expected to undertake repetitive testing to simulate stress and capacity which verification will not. On the other hand, verification is designed to test many boundary conditions or corner cases that normal quality assurance testing does not reach.

The thoroughness with which verification is undertaken is determined by a number of factors and the assessment of how thoroughly an assertion should be verified is a matter for individual decision. In some cases, the complexity of the verification software needed to test all combinations of cases may outweigh the value of testing, a carefully chosen subset of combinations often provides sufficient information. Similarly, it is important to verify aspects of the definition that are most likely to be used in the development of applications rather than entering into costly developments to verify corner cases.

## TESTABILITY ISSUES

There are many cases in which the testability of an assertion is either not possible or no test method is currently devised. The limitation of verification to software test methods makes it impossible to test deterministically in certain areas. For example, software verification of terminal line speeds is not fully determinable, but some measure of line speed change can be determined by the use of software tools.

In certain cases, testing is limited by the hardware available and where implementation does not provide support, the verification suite needs to correctly report the limitations imposed upon it.  In other cases, the definitions in the standard may not provide enough information to allow a test to be developed in a standard way, it may be necessary to invoke implementation-specific routines in order to test certain assertions.  Again the verification suite must act consistently in cases where these implementation-specific facilities are not available.

The criteria chosen when developing a verification suite may also effect testability. A major issue in this area is the portability of the verification suite; there is a trade-off between portability and testability.  For example, a suite designed to execute on one particular microprocessor can make architectural assumptions that a suite destined for a wider audience cannot make.


## TEST METHOD DEVELOPMENT

In developing test methods for standards verification, a certain degree of conformance of the underlying system must be assumed. These assumptions are normally undocumented but are based on the understanding that the system being verified has undergone basic quality assurance procedures and that the verification suite is unlikely to find errors in fundamental areas.

Care must be taken in test method development to avoid any precedence problems that may occur and to ensure that the test method is appropriate for the assertion being tested.  Any inter-dependencies between tests must be carefully avoided in order to ensure the validity of the test results.

It is often necessary to make assumptions when developing test methods, particularly in the area of timeliness of events. This is an area in which standards do not always specify the interval during which an event must occur and it is left to the designer of the verification suite to assess what is reasonable.

The normal method of executing a verification suite will accept that the user will not want to interact sporadically with the suite.  Any areas in which user interaction is necessary need to be isolated and executed as a separate part of the execution process. This allows a user to leave the verification suite to execute while undertaking other work or after a day's work has been completed.

## TEST RESULTS

While the simple principle of reporting a test, and subsequently an implementation, as having passed or failed, this is often not an adequate determination in the case of complex standards. The cases where a particular option is not implemented or the hardware configuration under test does not provide the facilities need to be separately identified. Also there is a need from the implementors point of view to distinguish tests which could not be executed because of a problem during test set up from those which failed during execution of the aspect being tested.

The reporting demands from the system implementor differ from those required by other verification suite users. The former group of users are interested in locating the error in their implementation and require as much information as necessary to correctly identify the problem. Other users are satisfied with much broader information on which to base their purchasing decisions. It is possible to use summary reports and debugging facilities to cater for both needs from the same verification suite.

## TEST STRUCTURES

The construction of a verification suite requires the development of user interfaces and standard software to allow the suite to execute on the target environment. These elements are often referred to as Configuration and Driver software.

A typical verification suite will consist of five elements. Firstly, configuration which captures user information concerning the facilities available on the system being tested. Secondly, installation which uses the configuration parameters to install the basic software used in the remainder of the verification process. Thirdly, building the test cases using the software tools provided on the system. Fourthly, executing the test cases on the target system and, finally, reporting the results of the execution phase.

In constructing these basic software elements, the question of the skill level expected from the user must be carefully considered. The more complex the configuration details required to execute the suite, the less likely the user is to provide the required information. This may either result in tests being omitted or, worse still, in tests producing erroneous results. Verification software, by its very nature, is a complex tool which is being applied increasingly complex areas. The need for such software to be run by agencies has long been established, not only to ensure independence, but also to ensure correct execution.

It is important to ensure that the source code is not modified for different implementations. Any such changes need to be strictly controlled within a release procedure to ensure that equality is preserved.

While the use of independent agencies has been mentioned, it is also necessary for a manufacturer or implementor to be able to use the verification suite during software development. The need to execute tests that failed on previous runs and to produce full regression analysis is important to software developers and a good verification suite will provide these facilities.


## TESTING VERIFICATION SOFTWARE

The testing of verification software is one of the most important, and yet often most difficult processes. In almost every case of test failure, an implementor's instinct will be to investigate the test rather than the implementation. For this reason, a clear modular approach is needed in the construction of a verification suite, this assists both in testing the verification suite and in investigating failures.

Often in producing verification software, the implementation itself is non-conforming with the standard being verified. In these cases, the use of traditional methods, such as producing software to simulate the facility being tested, can be used. The danger in testing verification software is the test that incorrectly asserts system behaviour to be successful when this is not the case. Such problems are often difficult to detect and even building a specifically non-conforming system can fail to detect such an error.

In many ways, the most exhaustive form of testing is allowing the verification suite to be executed on a wide range of platforms. This technique will help to identify a case where assumptions have been made in the test method, identify faults in the verification software (especially subtle timing issues) and determine  consistency of failures across different ranges of hardware. The last of these cases may cause some feedback into the standard itself where behaviour is incorrectly described.

## THE APPLICATION OF VERIFICATION SOFTWARE

Verification software is targeted for the benefit of both the manufacturer or system implementor and the equipment buyer. In the latter case, the process of competitive tendering may use verification software to ensure that the facilities provided are compatible with requirements. A software developer may use verification to ensure that products can be transferred to the new environment.

The manufacturer and system implementor, on the other hand, will use verification suites as part of their normal quality assurance cycle. As end-users demand proof of conformance during the tendering process, the manufacturers will become increasingly aware of the usefulness and necessity of verification.

The use of verification suites to police the market for Open Systems is set to become an increasing reality during the next few years. The industry is looking towards proven compatibility, the assurances of the manufacturers will no longer be considered satisfactory, and attempts to deviate from industry standards will not be tolerated.

## WORDS OF CAUTION

It must be stressed that verification software is not enough to determine conformance. There are limits to the extent of any verification suite and success only provides an indication of conformance.

There are problems in dealing with ranges of machines where a manufacturer has verified one machine in the range and expects that all of the others are conforming. The end-user needs to make himself aware of the exact architecture on which conformance was measured. Likewise, there may be problems with software releases and upgrades which have not been verified by the manufacturer.

The only answer to this problem is to ensure that any statement of conformance is carefully worded, providing a purchaser with adequate information about the specific implementation that has been tested.

## CONCLUSION

Undoubtedly the demand for Open Systems and the associated requirement for standards are here to stay. The international standards bodies are having an increasingly important role in today's computing industry, with industry agreed software standards being developed in a wide range of areas. The areas addressed are being dictated by the large users with a wide range of software elements being included in their Common Application Environment or Application Portability Profile.

In parallel with the development of the standards is a requirement from the user that there should be a measurement of conformance to the defined standard. The user is no longer going to be satisfied with the manufacturers promise that a system conforms to a standard but will demand that there is a measure of conformance provided through verification. The demand for products which have been verified will increase in parallel with the user demand for Open Systems.

# Glossary

**ACSE**    (Association Control Service Element) An entity in the application layer which handles the connections between applications running on Open Systems.

**ANSI**    (American National Standards Institute) The US standards body; a contributor to ISO.

**AOWS**    (OSI Asian and Oceanic Workshop) A forum for the development of OSI profiles and conformance testing specifications. Similar in purpose to EWOS in Europe.

**Application**    A user program that runs at the top level in a computer system and performs some useful task, such as wordprocessing.

**Application layer**    The top layer in the ISO OSI seven-layer model that provides the interface between the OSI environment and the application. The application layer is not an application program, but provides a link from applications, through the OSI environment, to applications on other systems.

**Architecture**    The structure of a network or system, including the hardware and software. The architecture includes definitions of the functions, interfaces between functions and protocols for communicating between functions.

**BSI**    (British Standards Institute) The British standards body; a contributor to ISO.

**Base standard**    A term used to distinguish basic international data communications standards from functional standards (or profiles) which are directed to a more specific user community.

**Bus**    A connection topology used in LANs such as Ethernet and in computer hardware. All messages go to all nodes on the bus, but only the node that is addressed will respond.

| | |
|---|---|
| CADDIA | Cooperation in Automation of Data and Documentation for Import/Export and Agriculture. An EC programme aimed at implementing electronic exchange between the Commission and member States. |
| CCITT | (International Consultative Committee on Telephony and Telegraphy) The United Nations agency that makes recommendations regarding telecommunications. Mainly consists of PTTs. |
| CCR | (Commitment, Concurrency and Recovery Service Element) An application layer element providing procedures for ensuring the integrity of a set of operations, possibly involving application processes in a number of systems. For example, in the operation of the JTM procedures. |
| CCTA | (Central Computer and Telecommunications Agency) An internal technical advisory centre for the UK government and related bodies. |
| CEN | (European Committee for Standardisation) The official standards body of the European Community. |
| CENELEC | (European Committee for Electrotechnical Standardisation) The European electrical standards body. The counterpart of the international body, the IEC. |
| CEPT | (European Conference on Posts and Telecommunications) The committee of European telecoms operators; the counterpart of the CCITT. |
| Connectionless | A mode of communication between systems in which connections are not held for the duration of communication. |
| Connection-oriented | A mode of communication between systems in which the connection is held for the duration of communication. For example, circuit switched networks such as the telephone system. |
| COS | (Corporation of Open Systems) A group of mainly American manufacturers who have agreed to promote Open Systems and develop conformance tests. |

| | |
|---|---|
| COSINE | Cooperation for Open Systems Interconnection Networking in Europe. |
| CSMA/CD | (Carrier Sense Multiple Access, Collision Detect) A LAN protocol. When two systems try to use the LAN at the same time, they both back off, wait for a random interval and then try again. |
| Data Link layer | Layer 2 of the ISO OSI seven-layer model. Synchronises transmission and handles error correction. |
| De facto standards | Solutions to computing or communications problems that are widely adopted, but not controlled by a public standards body. For example, the MS-DOS operating system for PCs. |
| ECMA | (European Computer Manufacturers' Association) A trade association of European computer manufacturers concerned with standards and other issues. |
| EDI | (Electronic Data Interchange) A set of standard data formats for information exchange which could eliminate much of the inter-company paperwork involved in raising orders and invoices. |
| EDIFACT | A United Nations' initiative to establish international standards for EDI. |
| Electronic mail | Interpersonal communication using computers or other IT equipment. CCITT X.400 is the electronic mail standard for Open Systems. |
| EMUG | European MAP User Group. |
| ESPRIT | (European Strategic Programme of Research in Information Technology) A European programme aimed at promoting the development and application of IT. |
| Ethernet | A type of LAN in which access to the bus is decided by the CSMA/CD protocol. The ISO or IEEE 802.3 standard for Ethernet is widely adopted by manufacturers. |

EurOSInet A group of IT suppliers that promote Open Systems, mainly by mounting demonstrations of OSI capabilities.

EWOS (European Workshop on Open Systems) A forum within the overall structure of CEN/CENELEC for the development of OSI profiles and conformance testing specifications.

ETSI (European Telecommunications Standards Institute) A forum within the overall structure of CEN/CENELEC for consideration of the telecommunications aspects of functional standardisation.

FDDI (Fibre Distributed Data Interface) A standard for high-speed optical fibre local area networks.

Feeders' Forum The name given to the collaboration between SPAG, COS, POSI and the world-wide MAP/TOP User Groups to promote the harmonisation of the various national and regional OSI initiatives.

FTAM (File Transfer, Access and Management) The OSI application layer standard that defines how files can be transferred, accessed and manipulated from a remote system.

Functional standard or profile A selection from the options within one or more OSI standard. Functional standards are designed to simplify the task of developing usable interoperating systems for particular applications.

Gateway A link between two networking architectures (for example, OSI and a proprietary network) that passes and translates messages from one to the other. If between two OSI networks, it is properly called a relay.

GOSIP Functional standards defined by government to make it easier for government departments to specify and procure Open Systems. Both UK and US GOSIPs exist.

Graphics standards Standards that allow images or information in a graphical form to be exchanged among Open Systems. For example, the Graphics Kernel System (GKS).

| | |
|---|---|
| Harmonisation | Adapting standards, profiles or conformance tests so that they agree. |
| HCI | (Human Computer Interface) That part of a system with which humans interact, usually based on terminal/keyboard and mouse. |
| IEC | (International Electrotechnical Commission) A standards body dealing with electrical systems. The overlap between ISO and IEC has been resolved by the formation of joint committees. |
| IEEE | (Institute of Electrical and Electronics Engineers) A US professional body involved in standards making, especially for LANs. |
| INSIS | Integrated Services Information System. An EC programme aimed at implementing electronic exchange between institutions and member states. |
| ISDN | (Integrated Services Digital Network) A digital network that can carry voice and data transmissions simultaneously. |
| ISP | (International Standardised Profile) See Functional standard. |
| IT | (Information Technology) The use of electronic equipment to handle information. |
| Interconnection | Linking systems together so that data can be passed between them - a more basic achievement than interworking. |
| Interworking | Linking systems together so that application processes can communicate effectively with each other. |
| ISO | (International Standards Organisation) The body that decides on international standards. Standards are decided by committees of representatives from industry nominated by the standards bodies of the different countries. |
| JTM | (Job Transfer and Manipulation) The OSI application layer standard that allows jobs to be submitted to remote machines over an OSI link. |

LAN             (Local Area Network) A system providing data communications over a small area, for example a building or a campus.

LLC1            (Logical Link Control 1) A Stardard for part of the data link layer providing control of data transfer over an established connection.

MAP             (Manufacturing Automation Protocol) An OSI-based functional standard, set by the MAP Users' Group, led by General Motors, for open systems interconnection in manufacturing. Closely related to TOP.

MHS             (Message Handling Service) The ISO nomenclature for electronic mail.

Migration       The adaptation of a user's system from proprietary protocols to Open Systems standards, usually by stages over a period of years.

MOTIS           (Message Oriented Text Interchange System) ISO (10021) version of X.400 electronic mail systems.

NBS             (National Bureau of Standards) A US government body involved in standards activities.

Network layer   The third layer of the OSI model. Establishes connections and arranges routes from one system to another.

ODA             (Office Document Architecture) A standard for the format of documents to ensure that they are exchanged (via X.400 message handling services) in a format that can be handled by the receiving system.

ODP             (Open Distributed Computing) The distribution of interrelated processing tasks across a number of systems.

Open System     A system that is able to communicate with those from other vendors. The OSI model is generally regarded as the best route to Open Systems because it is independent of individual vendors.

| | |
|---|---|
| OSI | (Open Systems Interconnection) A strategy of adopting standard communications protocols, defined by the OSI reference model to be vendor-independent, so that Open Systems can be constructed. The OSI scheme is aimed at providing interworking as well as interconnection. |
| OSI reference model | The generic model by which Open Systems are constructed in OSI. Also known as the 'seven layer model' because the process of communication is divided into seven layers with standard interfaces between them. |
| OSInet | A multi-vendor demonstration network run by the US NBS. |
| OSITOP | The European users association for the promotion of useful computer communications stands. Established in February 1987, and currently has over 120 members, including major users from most of the European countries. |
| PABX | (Private Automatic Branch Exchange) A system that handles switching of voice (and sometimes data) connections on a subnetwork of telephone lines within a building. |
| Packet-switching | A method of sending data over wide area networks (WANs). Each message is broken into packets which are routed separately over the network and then recombined at the receiving system. X.25 is a packet-switched network. |
| Physical layer | The bottom layer of the OSI model. It handles the physical connection to a communication medium (i.e., wire or cable) and converts the data into a stream of signals suitable for the medium. |
| POSI | The Japanese OSI promotion group. |
| POSIX | The IEEE standard for a portable operating system. It is based on UNIX. |
| Presentation layer | The sixth layer of the OSI model. It handles the syntax changes that may be necessary between systems. |
| Profile | See Functional standard. |

| | |
|---|---|
| Proprietary | A networking architecture or other product controlled by one manufacturer. If widely adopted, it may be referred to as a de facto standard. |
| Protocol | A rule or set of rules that govern the way systems interact. OSI provides a separate protocol for each layer. |
| PTT | A national post, telegraphy and telecommunications agency. For example, British Telecom in the UK. |
| RARE | Résaux Associes pour la Recherche Européenne. |
| Reference model | See OSI reference model. |
| Relay | An intermediate system that passes messages between two OSI systems. |
| ROSE | (Remote Operations Service Element) An application layer element providing procedures to support interactive operations between application processes. |
| RTSE | (Reliable Transfer Service Element) An application layer element providing procedures for recovery from end system failure during transmission. |
| Session Layer | The fifth layer in the OSI model. Co-ordinates the dialogue between application processes. |
| Slotted Ring | A ring structured LAN where access is controlled by making the ring look like a continuously circulating conveyor belt, If a slot is empty any station may place data in it as it goes past. |
| SME | (Society of Manufacturing Engineers) The US body that handles administration for the MAP/TOP Users Group. |
| SNA | (Systems Network Architecture) IBM's proprietary networking architecture. |
| SPAG | (Standards Promotion and Application Group) A consortium of European suppliers promoting Open Systems. The prime mover behind European work on functional standards. |

Sublayer

A subdivision of an OSI layer where there are clearly distinct functions contained in one layer. Layers 2 and 3 are commonly subdivided in this way.

Subnetwork

A network that forms one part of the link between two OSI systems. The same technology is used throughout a subnetwork.

TCP/IP

(Transmission Control Protocol/Internet Protocol) A de facto standard developed by the US Department of Defense that is widely adopted. It covers approximately the functions of layers 3 and 4.

Test house

An organisation that has developed or licensed test suites and provides a testing service, usually including conformance and interoperability testing.

Token

A logical or notional status which can be possessed by only one communications entity. Depending on the context it confers some rights on the holder such as permission to initiate data transfer.

Token Bus

A local area network where access to a broadcast cable is controlled by possession of "token". The ISO Token Bus standard generally specifies broadband cable, and is part of the MAP functional standard.

Token Ring

A ring-structured local area network where permission to send data is controlled by possession of a token. There is an ISO standard for Token Ring, and it is also promoted by IBM.

TOP

(Technical and Office Protocol) The functional standards being promoted by Boeing, designed for the office environment. TOP is closely related and complementary to MAP.

Topology

The layout of a network; its pattern of interconnections.

Transport Layer

The fourth layer in the OSI model. The Transport Layer packages the lower layer functions, masking the hardware complexity and providing a clear channel for the upper layers to use. There are five optional transport classes which provide different levels of service.

UNIX                   An operating system owned and developed by AT&T, but licensed to many if not all computer manufacturers. It is a de facto standard.

VT                     (Virtual Terminal) An OSI application layer standard that aims to allow remote terminal access to Open Systems.

WAN                    (Wide Area Network) A network that spans a wide area. For example, X.25 and public networks.

X.25                   The CCITT recommendations for connection to packet-switched wide area networks. It has been adopted as part of the OSI model.

X.400                  The CCITT recommendations for message handling (i.e., electronic mail). It has been adopted as part of the OSI model.

X/Open                 An originally European, but now world-wide group of computer manufacturers that seeks to define and promote standards for software portability between UNIX systems.